ISTANBUL DIARY
Peter Bialobrzeski

February 12 – February 18, 2023

Hartmann books

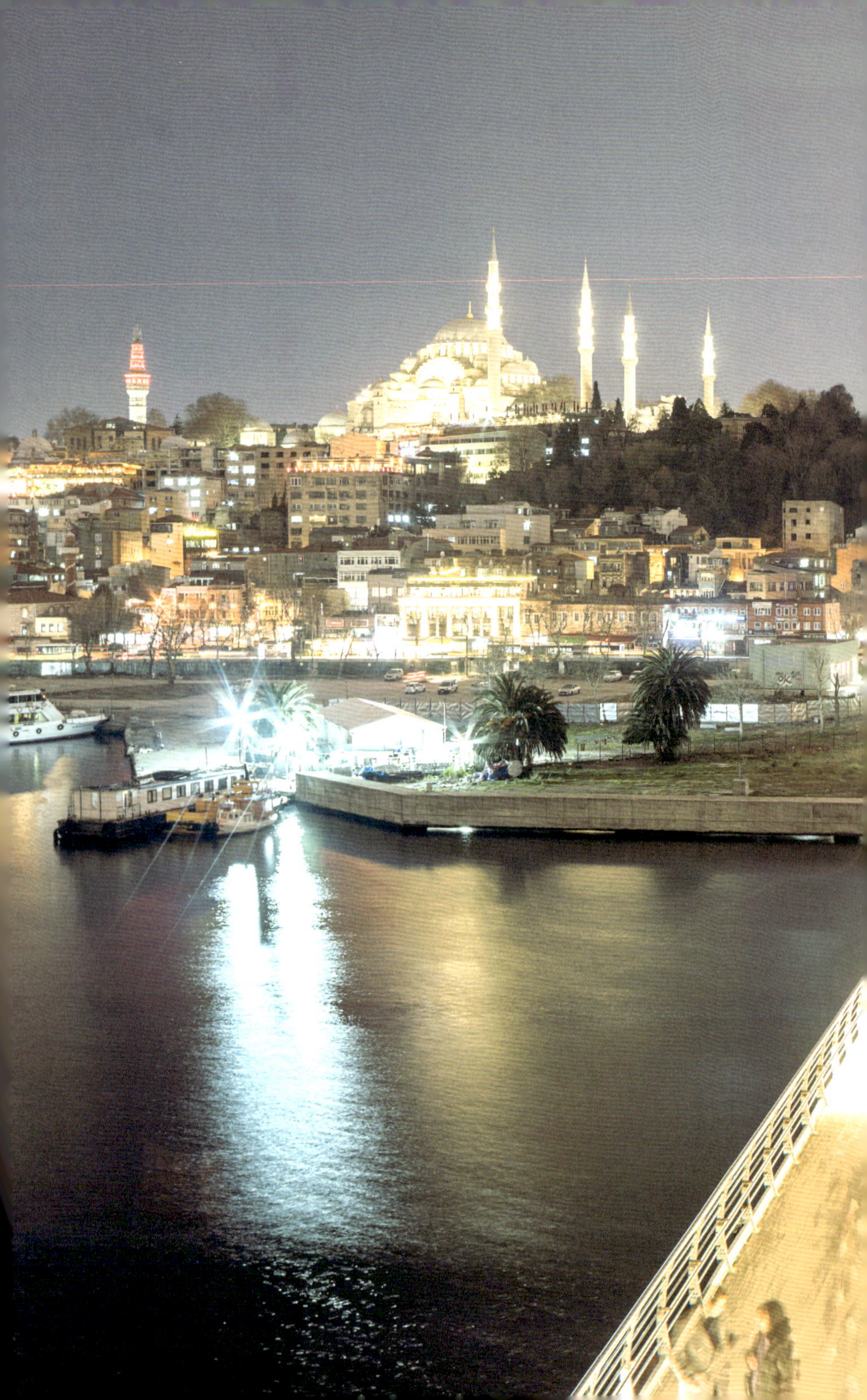

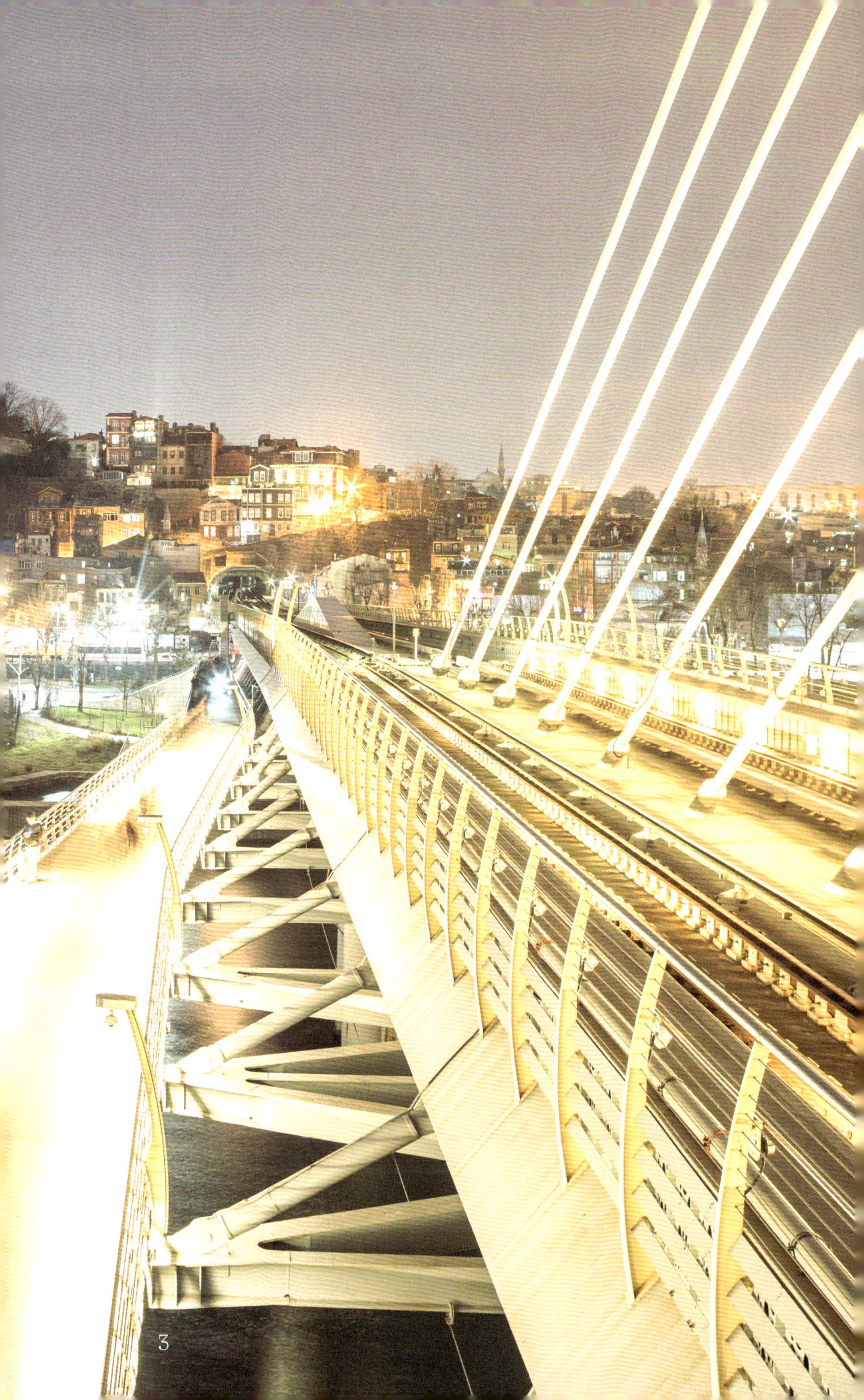

ISTANBUL DIARY
Peter Bialobrzeski

→ February 12, 2023 Bad start: I arrive two days late due to a canceled flight. "Bad weather," Turkish Airlines claims. I assume they were using the plane in connection with the earthquake that devastated parts of southeastern Turkey and northern Syria. Is it appropriate to go to a country where a large part of the population has lost loved ones in a disaster? Neither at the airport nor in the Beyoğlu district is there any sign of what happened. According to the English-language news site *Daily Sabah*, the death toll has risen to 24,600.

→ February 13, 2023 I had never heard of the Karlova zone where two fault lines meet according to Naci Görür, a geologist at Istanbul Technical University and a member of the Turkish Academy of Sciences. He warns that five million lives in Istanbul could be at stake. Experts say, "Istanbul, with a population of more than fifteen million, is Turkey's most populous city and is constantly at risk from earthquakes. Several studies show that the city will inevitably suffer from a strong earthquake. It is not a question of if, but when." According to the German news website *Tagesschau.de*, the death toll has risen to 28,000.

→ February 14, 2023 On the top floor of a mezze restaurant that occupies five floors of an old building, I meet a Turkish colleague from the German photo agency *laif*. Under the thin wooden roof, pipes blow hot air over our heads. I ask him if Turkey is still buying gas and oil from Putin. "Erdoğan is playing both sides," he replies. The death toll is 36,000.

→ February 15, 2023 The luxurious Peninsula Hotel is next to a noisy demolition site. I suspect that most guests would prefer my quiet, spacious apartment in Galata. On their way from the Peninsula, large, illuminated letters in glowing neon would tempt them to visit a shop called Cleopatra Ink-Tattoo and Piercing: “Make piercing, make art” along with the trending hashtag “Your body your choice.” The stock market reopens. The body count reaches 40,000.

→February 16, 2023 Even though the earthquake disaster in southeastern Turkey is not noticeable in my daily observations, I can’t help but imagine the unimaginable. What if the ground beneath my feet starts to shake? Going underground, especially at my local Şişhane station, where you can take up to eight elevators to descend into the hill, has lost its innocence.

→February 17, 2023 Innocence is not what the clothing vendors in Fatih could claim. From North Face and Moncler to Prada, you’ll find the same down jackets with prestigious labels. Down the road, on the larger streets, the gleaming façades and shop windows proudly display their own brand names: Daniel Gianni, Gabriel Moon, and Stefano Ragazzo—and that is just a small selection! People killed by the earthquake: 44,000.

→February 18, 2023 The district of Maslak, north of central Istanbul, seems to be home to all the car dealerships, spare parts dealers, and garages. From brand-new luxury cars to wrecked vehicles, these urban artifacts bear witness to a failed mobility policy. Every plot of land is being turned into a Vale parking lot managed by local residents who make commuters pay good money to park their beloved machines on empty wasteland adjacent to the last remaining apartment block surrounded by mushrooming skyscrapers.

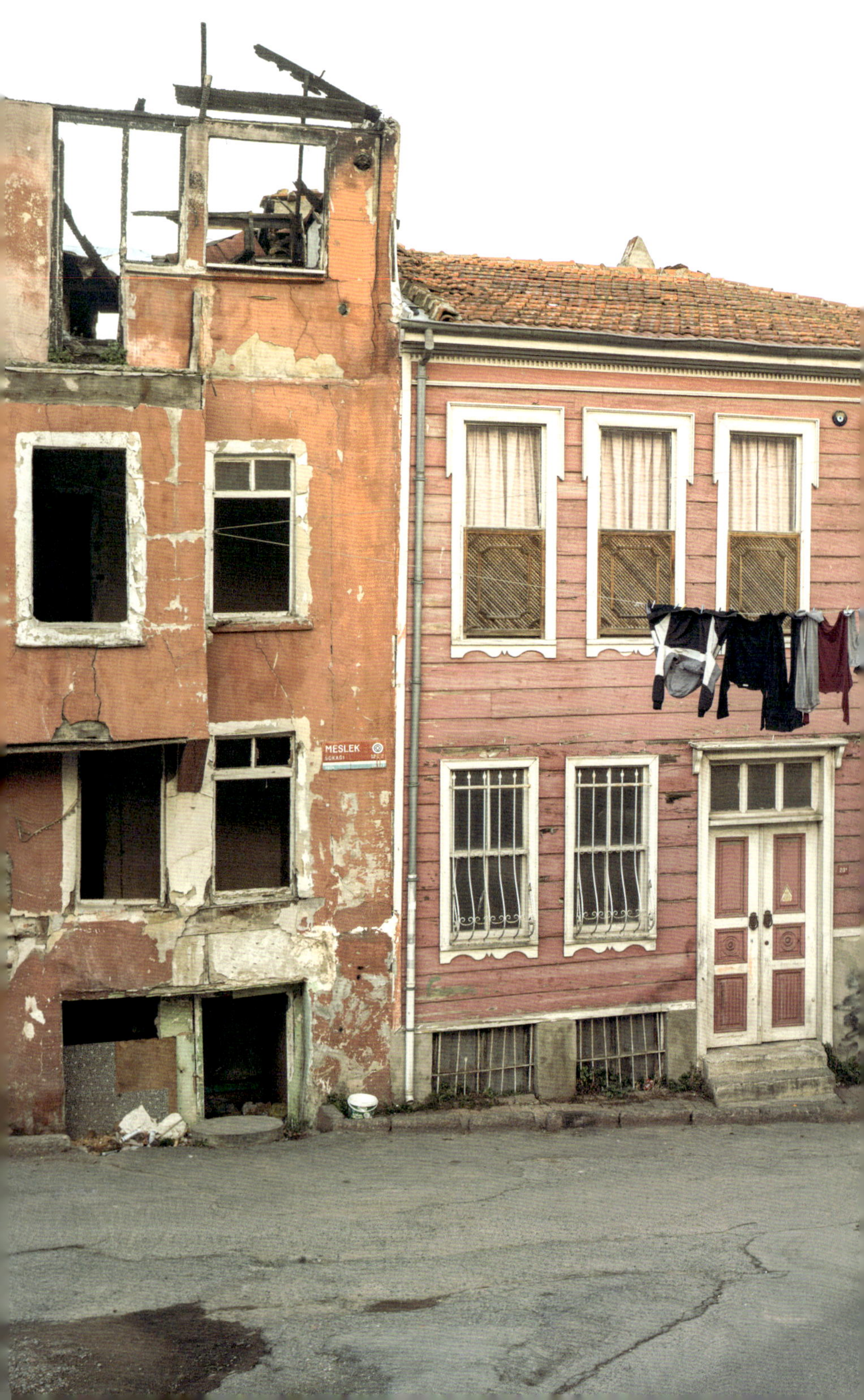
MESLEK
SOKAĞI

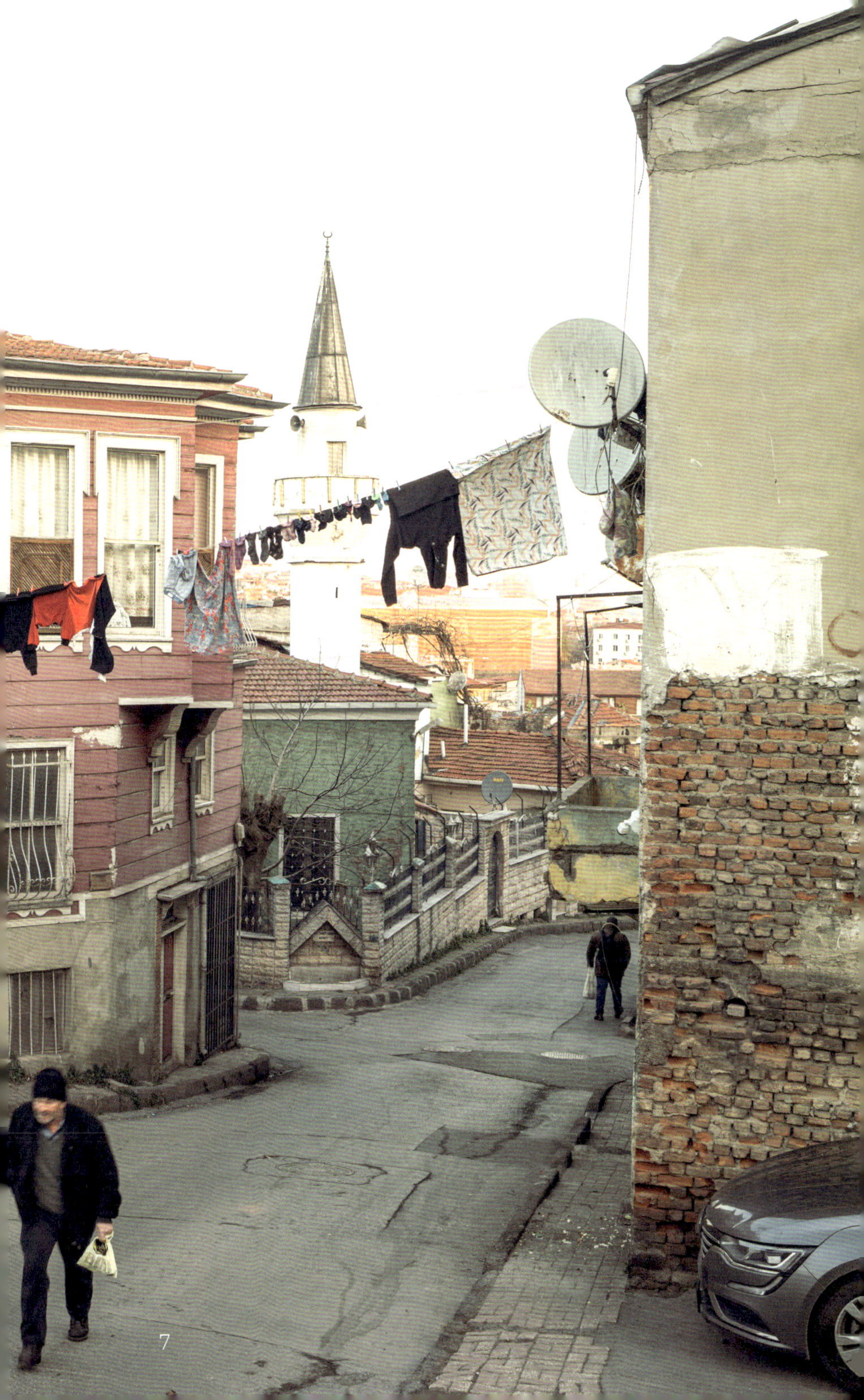

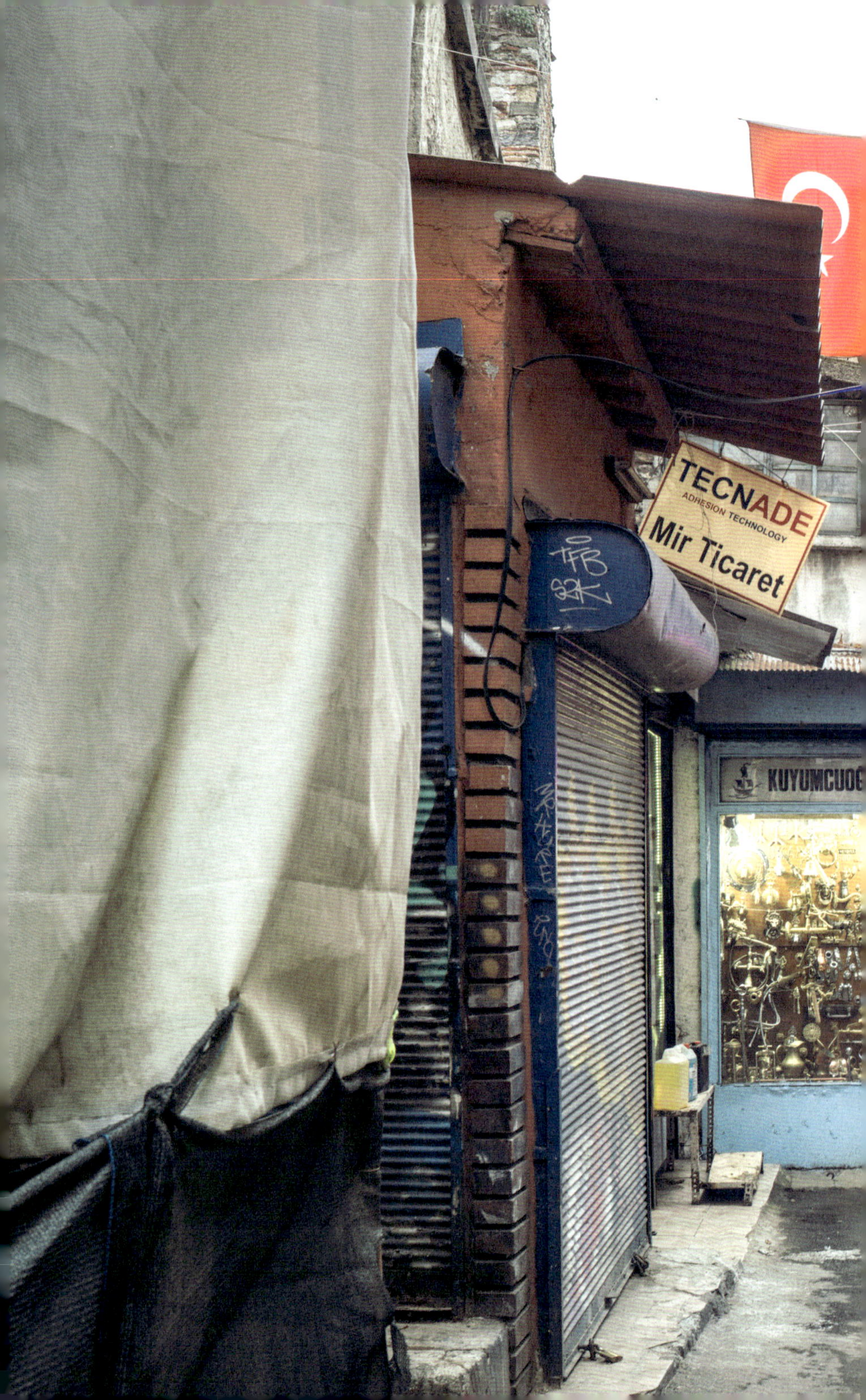
TECNADE
ADHESION TECHNOLOGY
Mir Ticaret
KUYUMCUOG

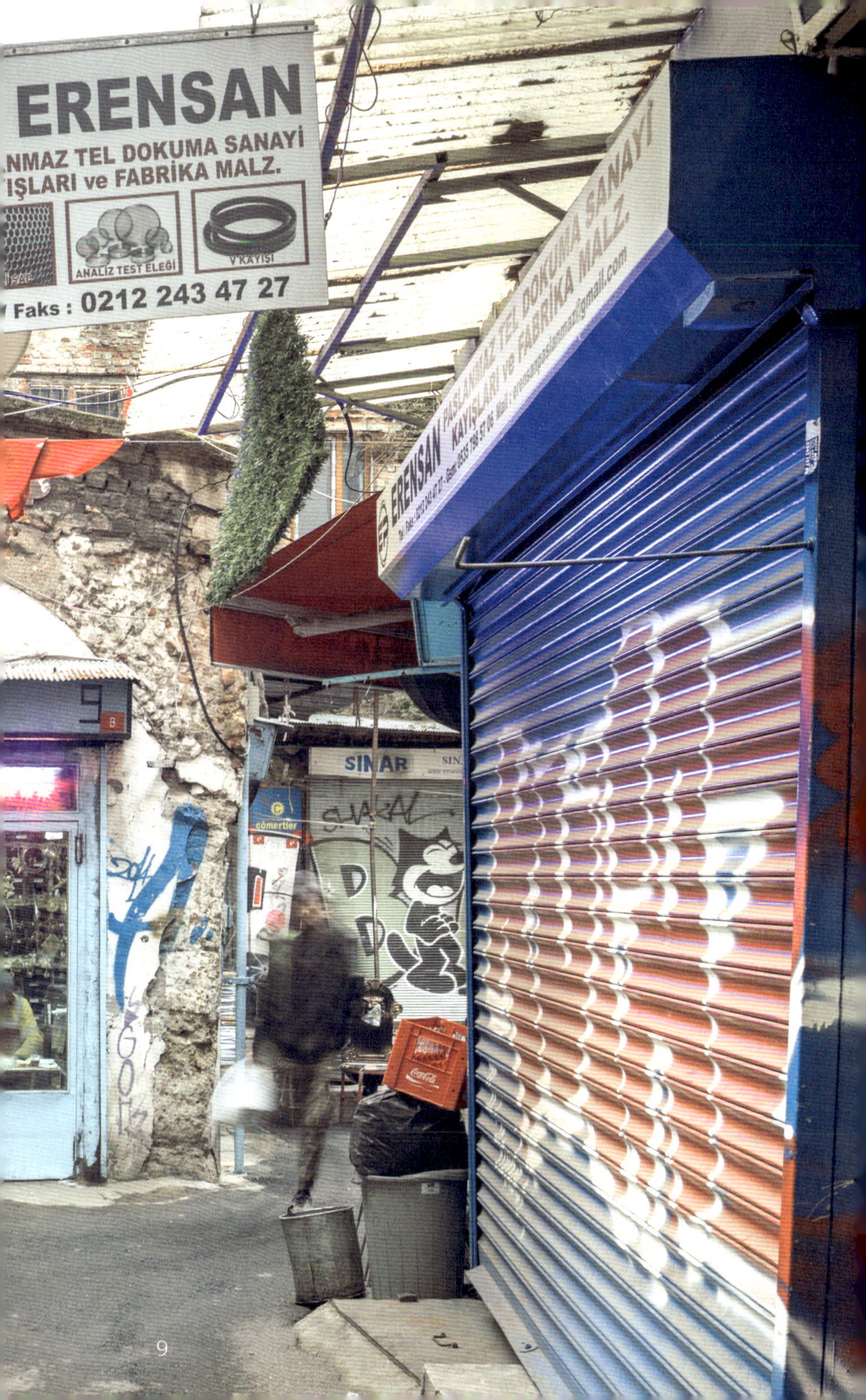

ERENSAN
NMAZ TEL DOKUMA SANAYİ
IŞLARI ve FABRİKA MALZ.
ANALİZ TEST ELEĞİ
V KAYIŞI
Faks : 0212 243 47 27
ERENSAN
PASLANMAZ TEL DOKUMA SANAYİ
KAYIŞLARI ve FABRİKA MALZ.
SINAR
cömertler
Coca-Cola

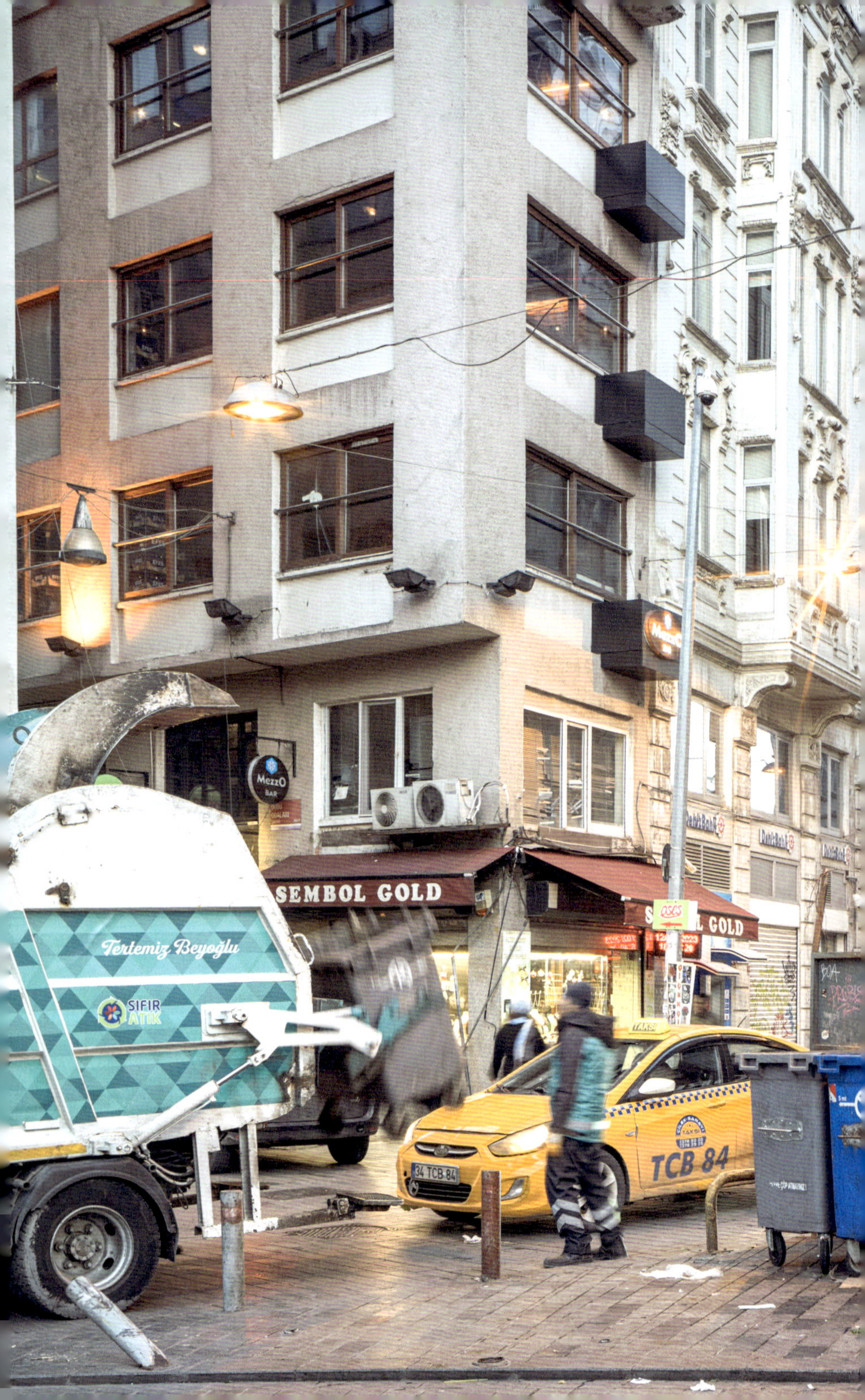

SEMBOL GOLD
Tertemiz Beyoğlu
SIFIR ATIK
MezzO
BAR
TCB 84
34 TCB 84

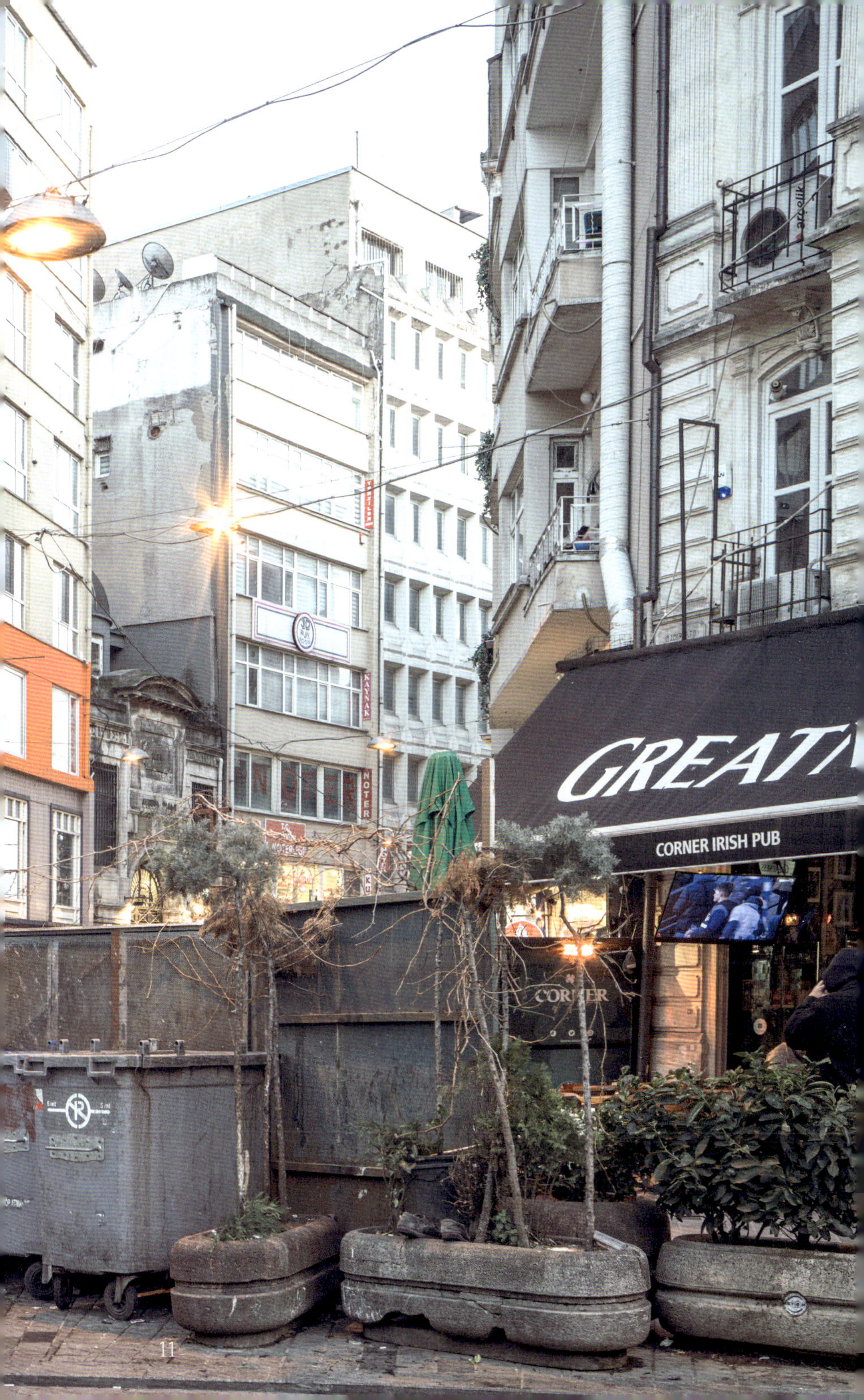
GREAT
CORNER IRISH PUB
NOTER
KAYNAK
CORNER

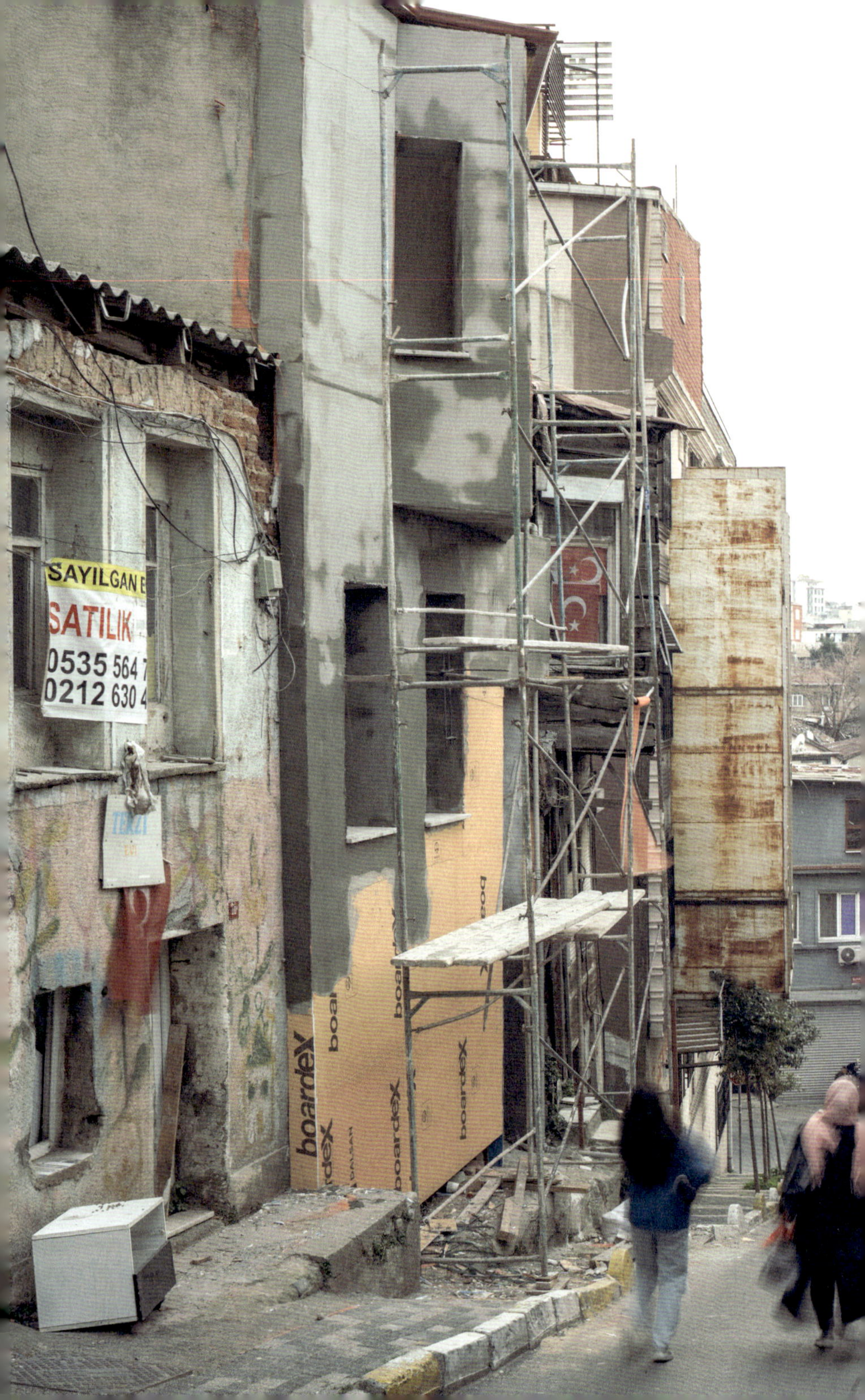
SAYILGAN E
SATILIK
0535 564 7
0212 630 4
TERZI
boardex

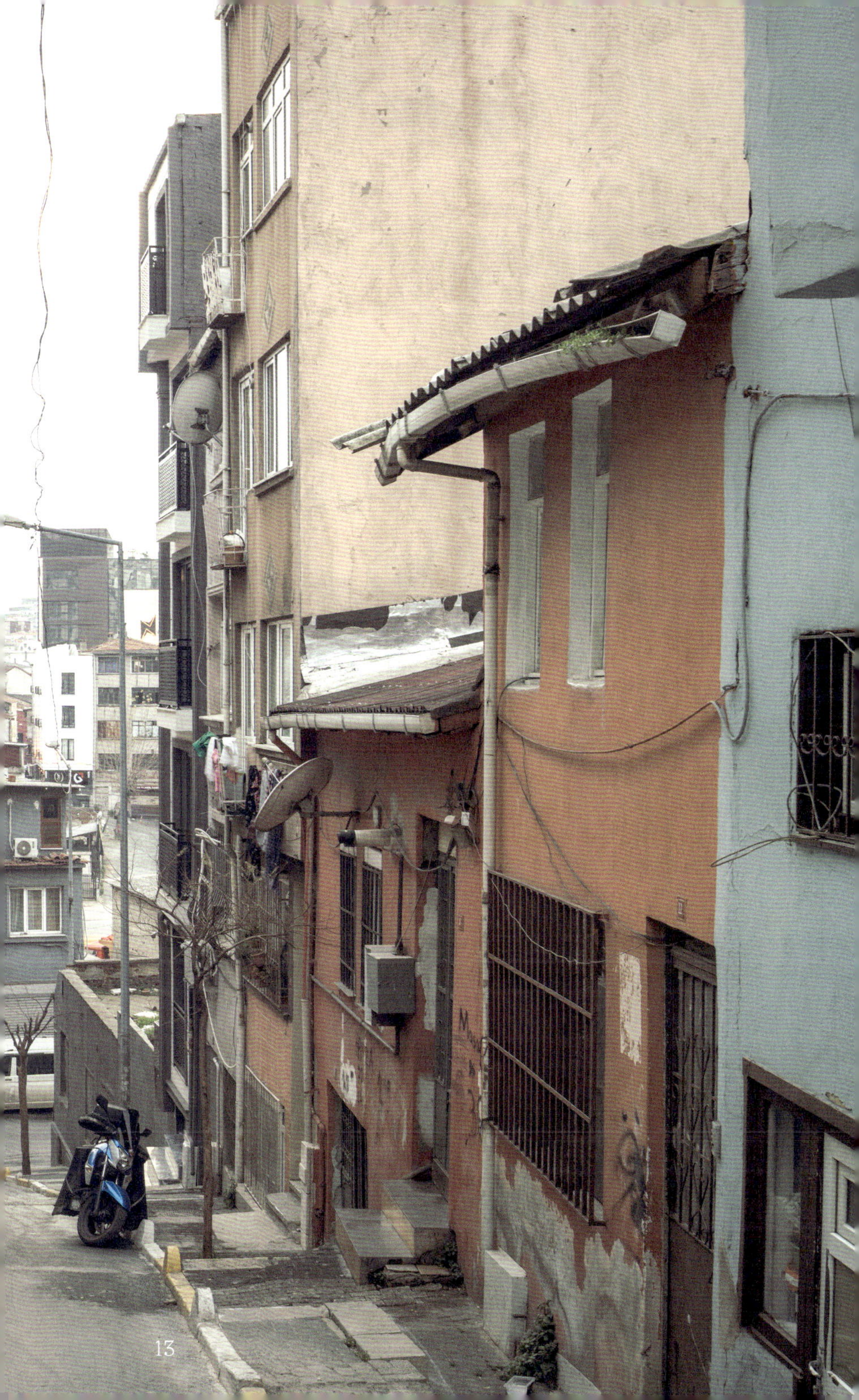

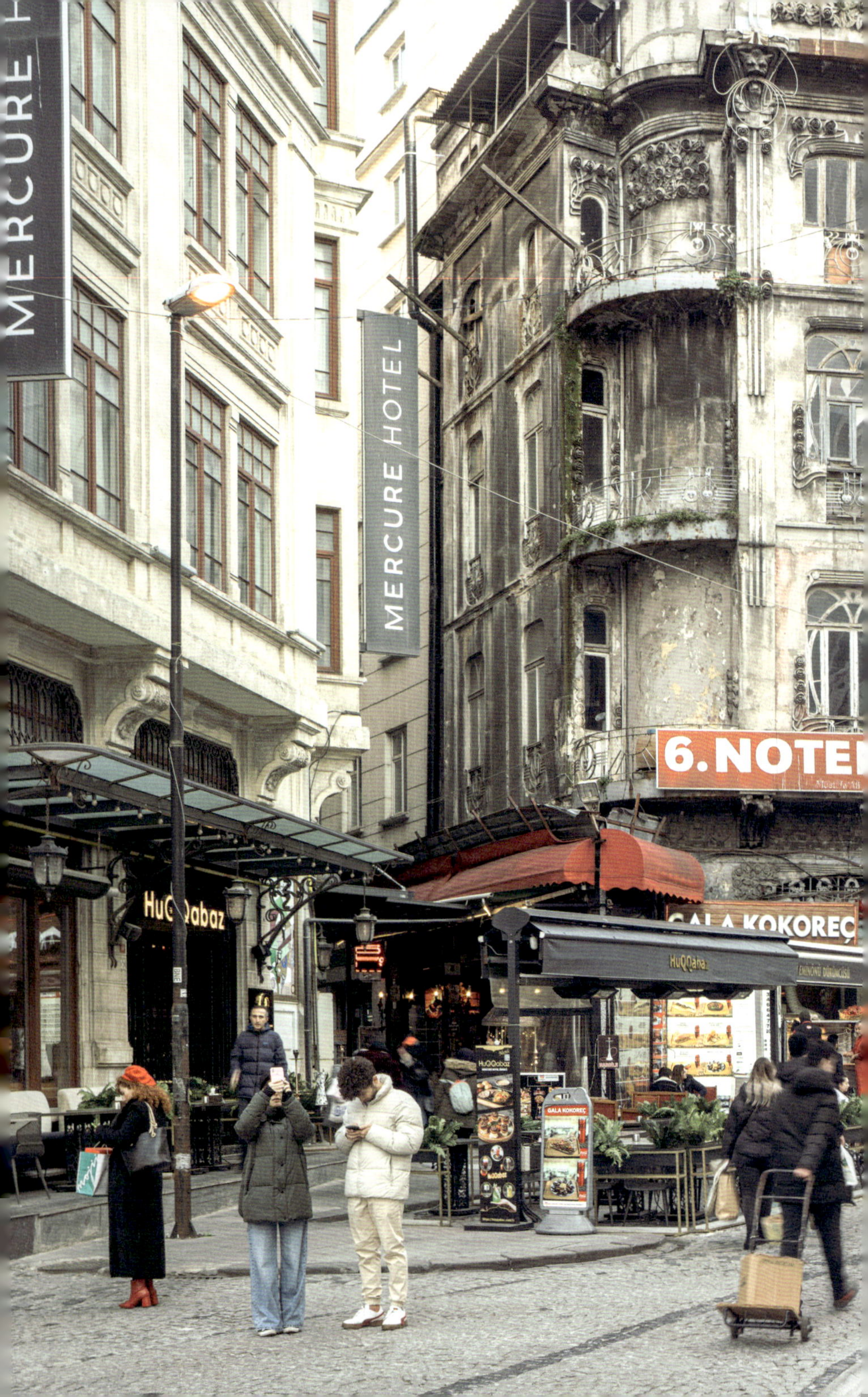
MERCURE H
MERCURE HOTEL
6. NOTE
HuQQabaz
GALA KOKOREÇ
HuQQaba

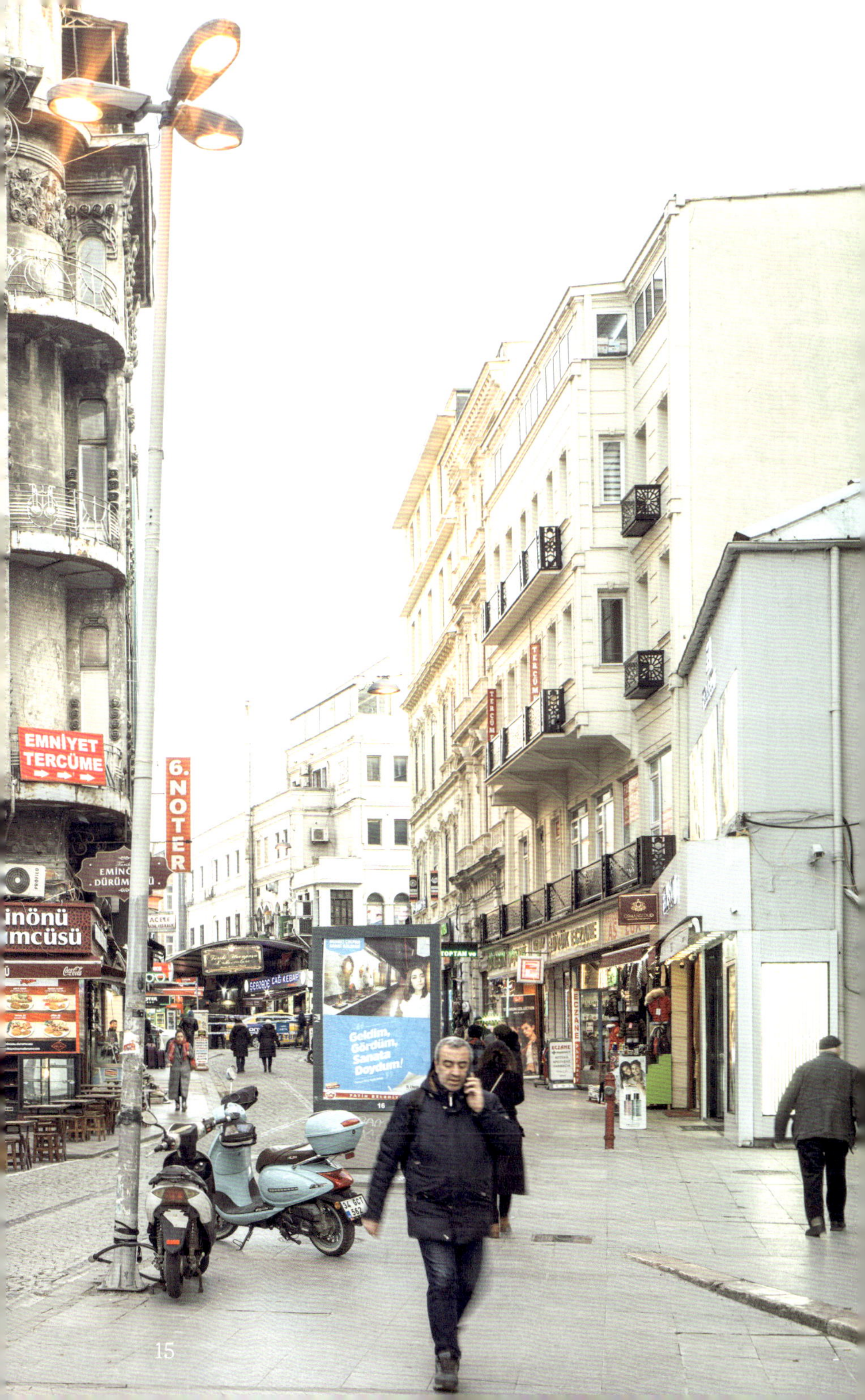
EMNİYET
TERCÜME
6. NOTER
TERCÜME
Geldim, Gördüm, Sanata Doydum!
TOPTAN
ECZANE

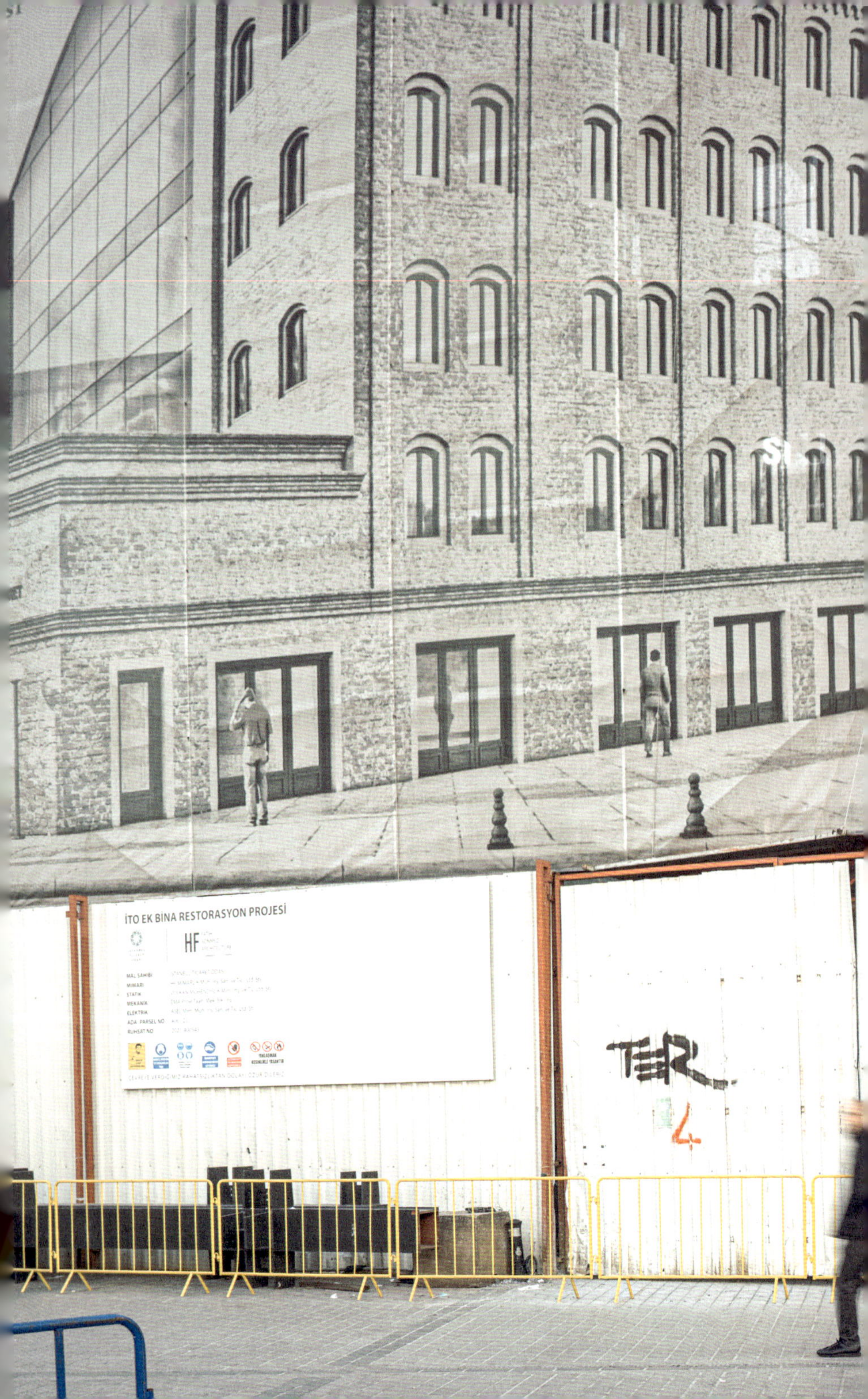
İTO EK BİNA RESTORASYON PROJESİ
HF

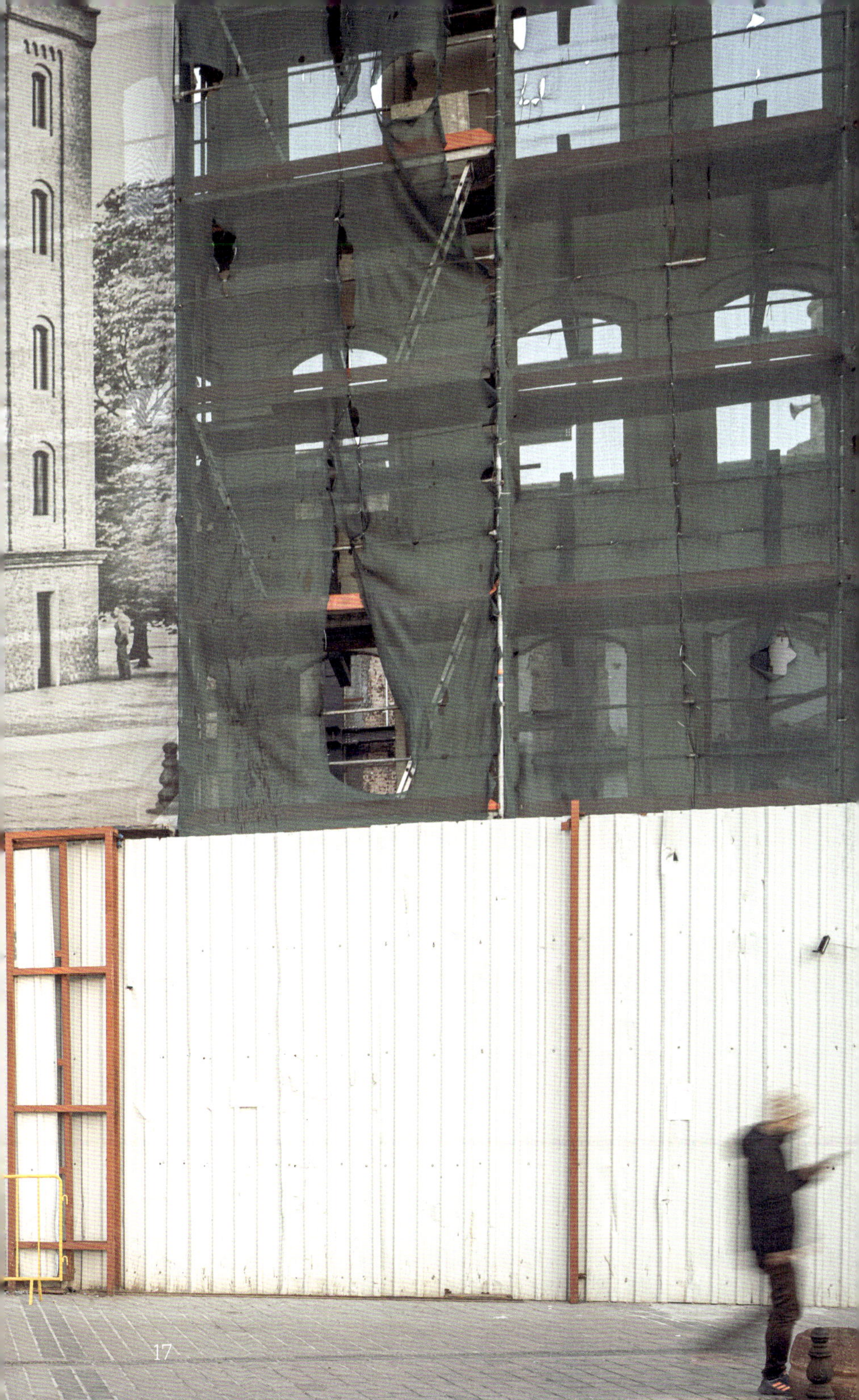

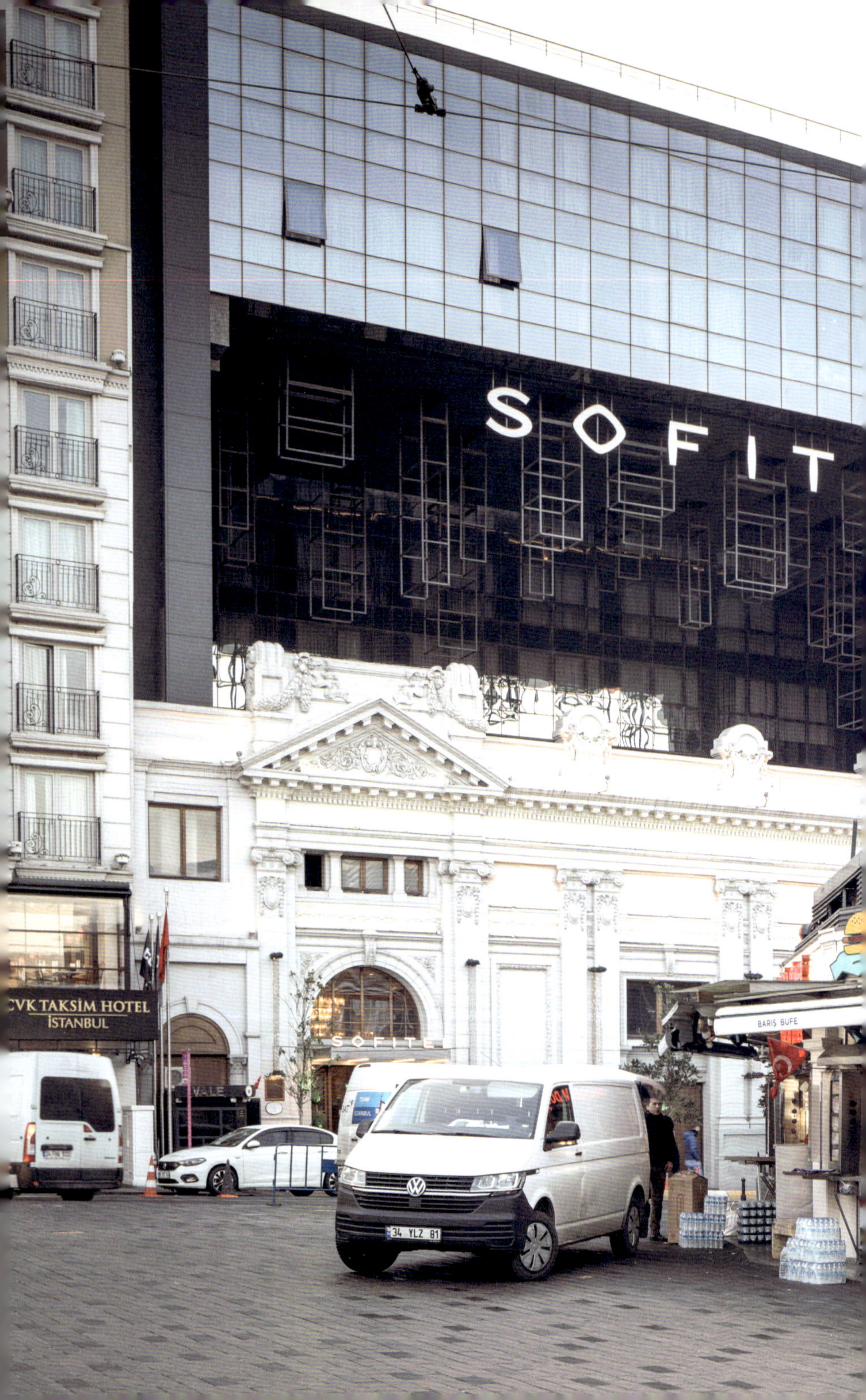
SOFIT
CVK TAKSIM HOTEL
İSTANBUL
SOFITE
BARIŞ BUFE
34 YLZ 81

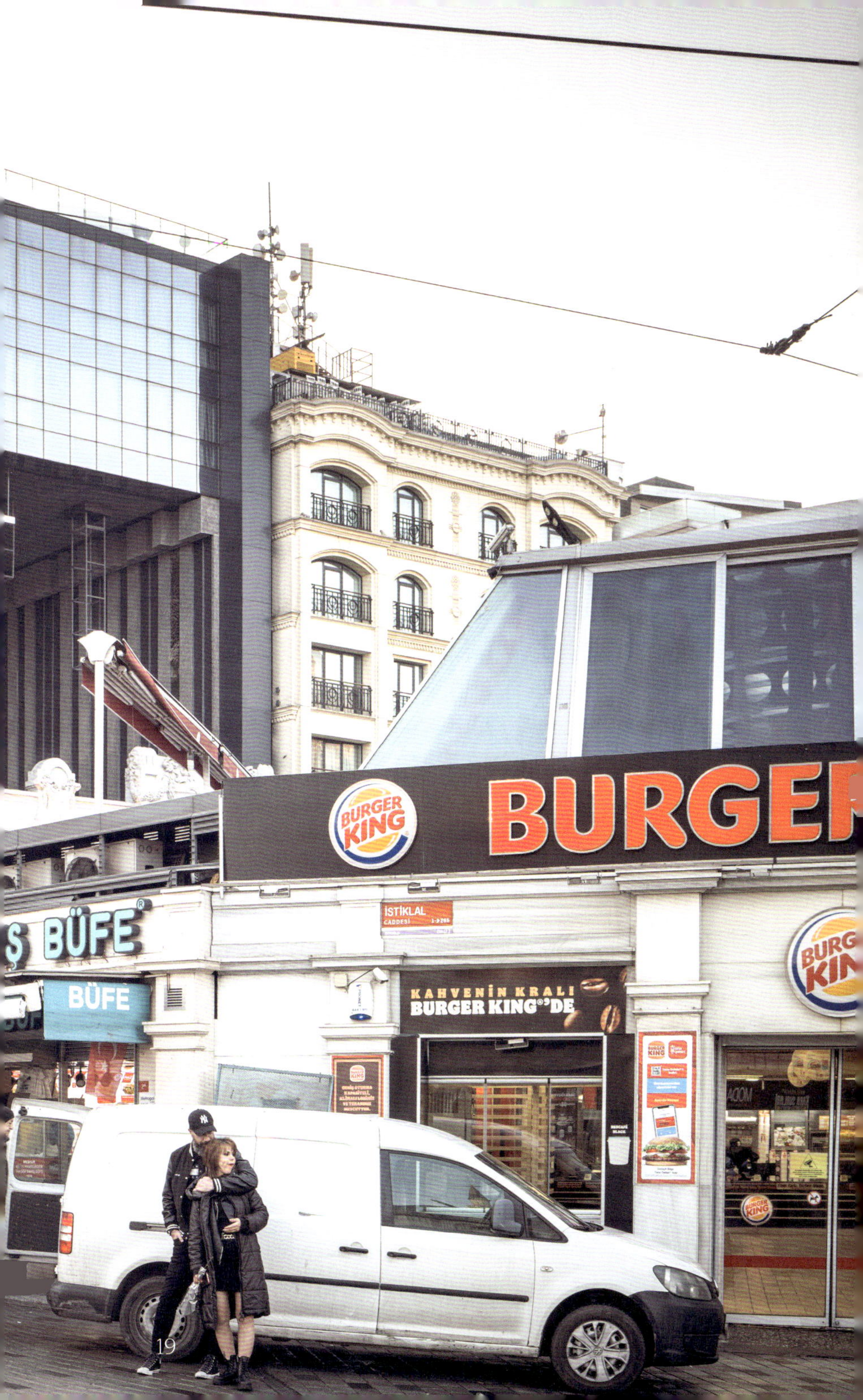
BURGER KING
BURGER
BÜFE
BÜFE
İSTİKLAL CADDESİ
KAHVENİN KRALI
BURGER KING®'DE

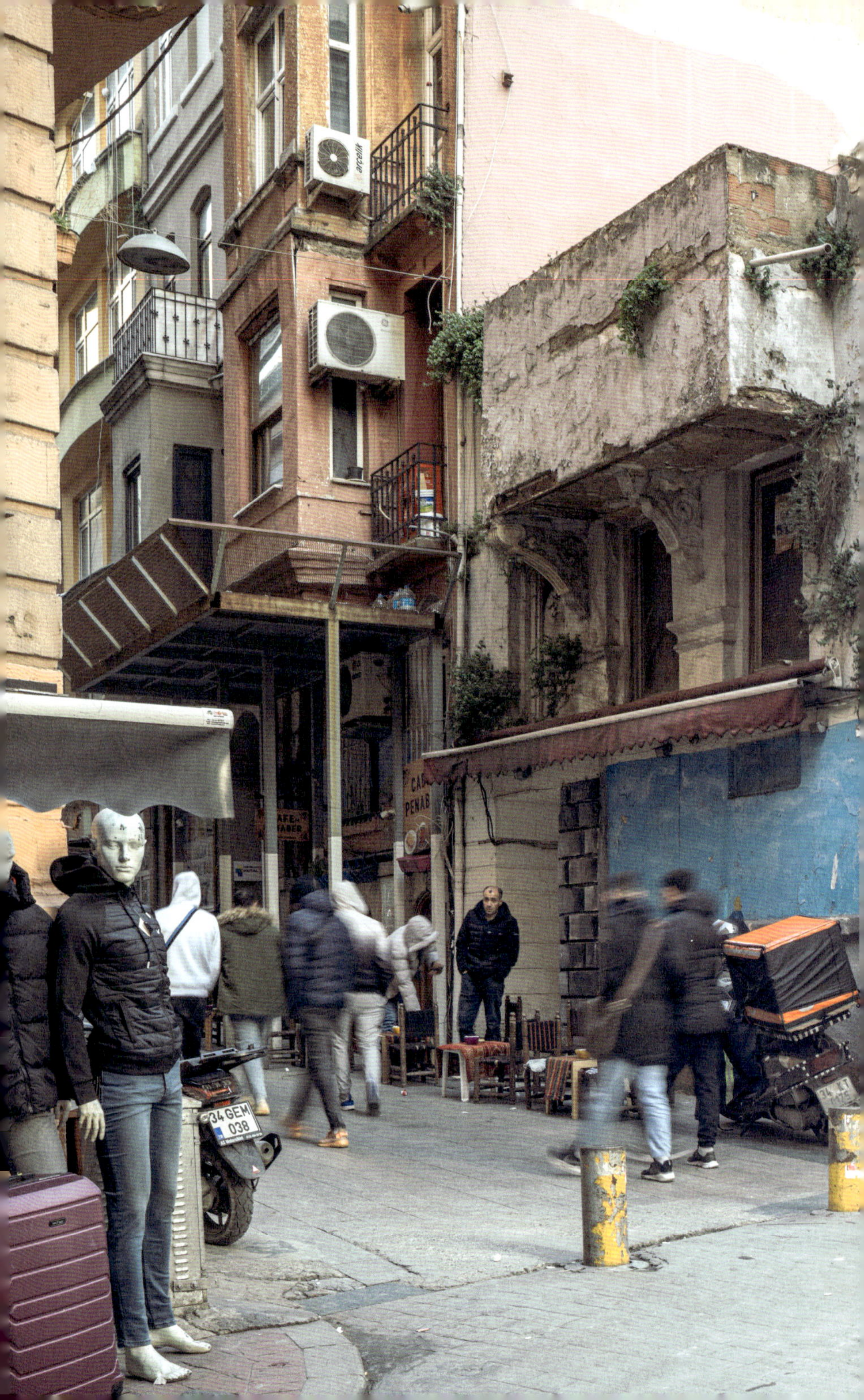
arçelik
34 GEM
038

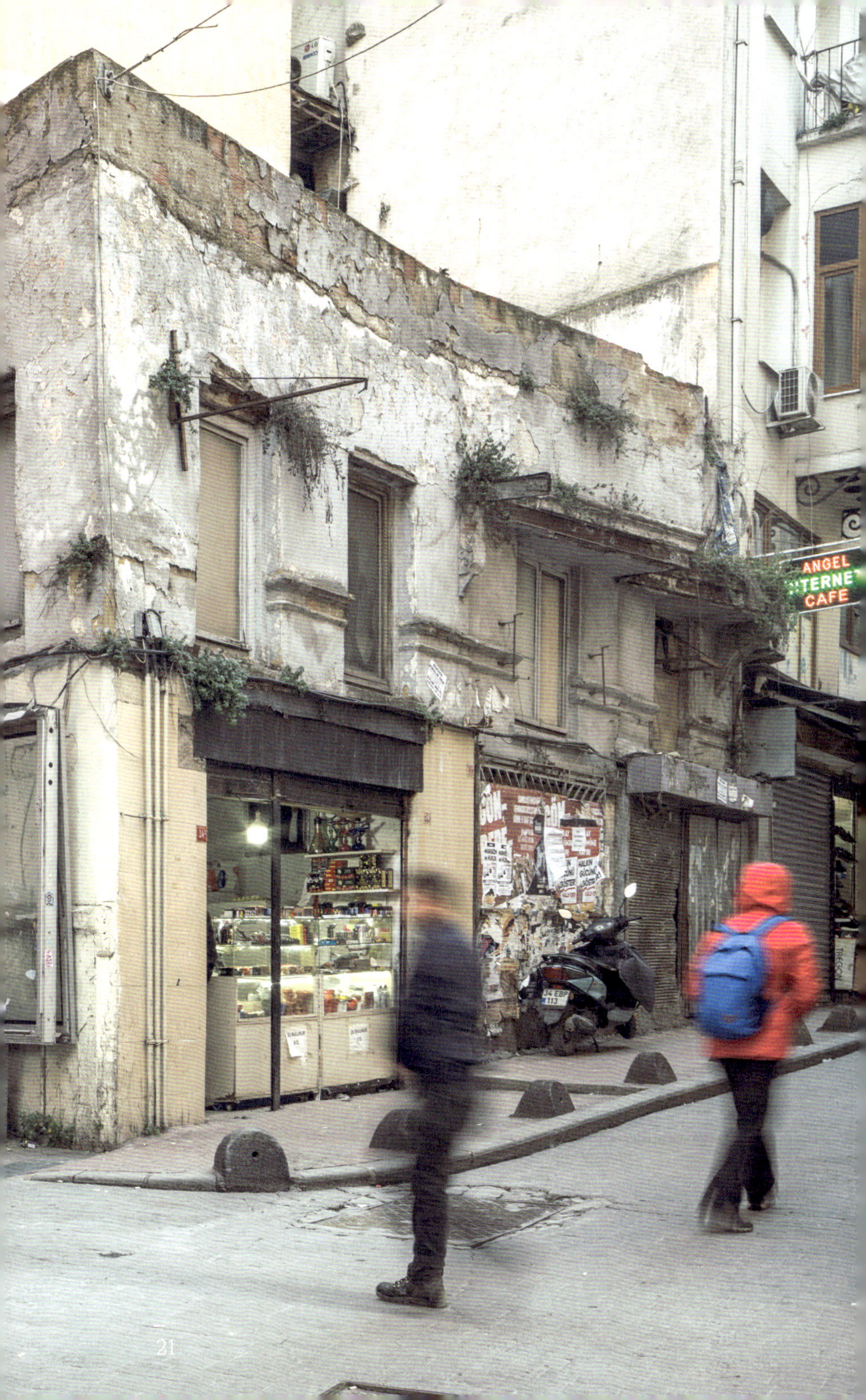
ANGEL
TERNE
CAFE
34 EBP
113

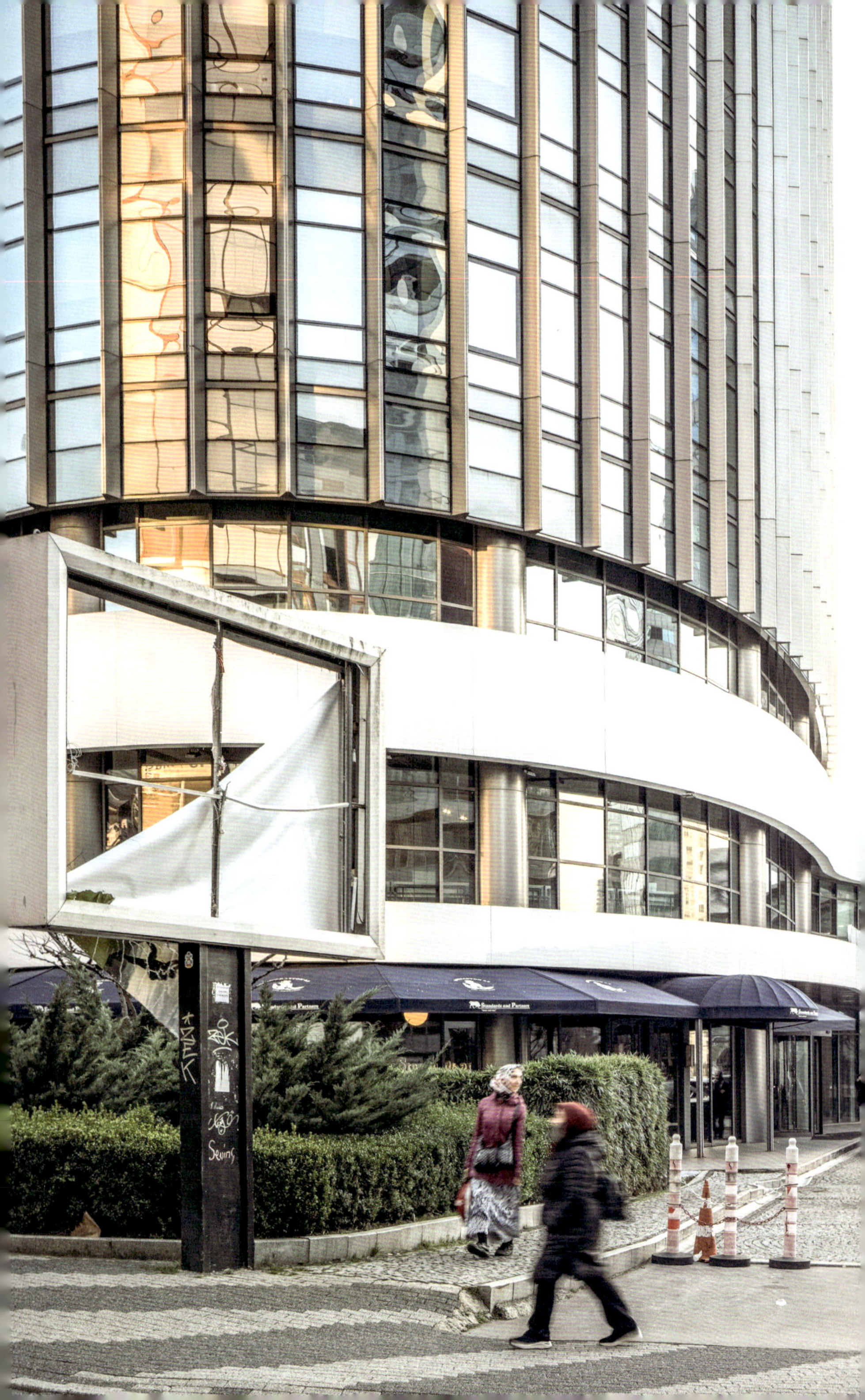
Standards and Partners

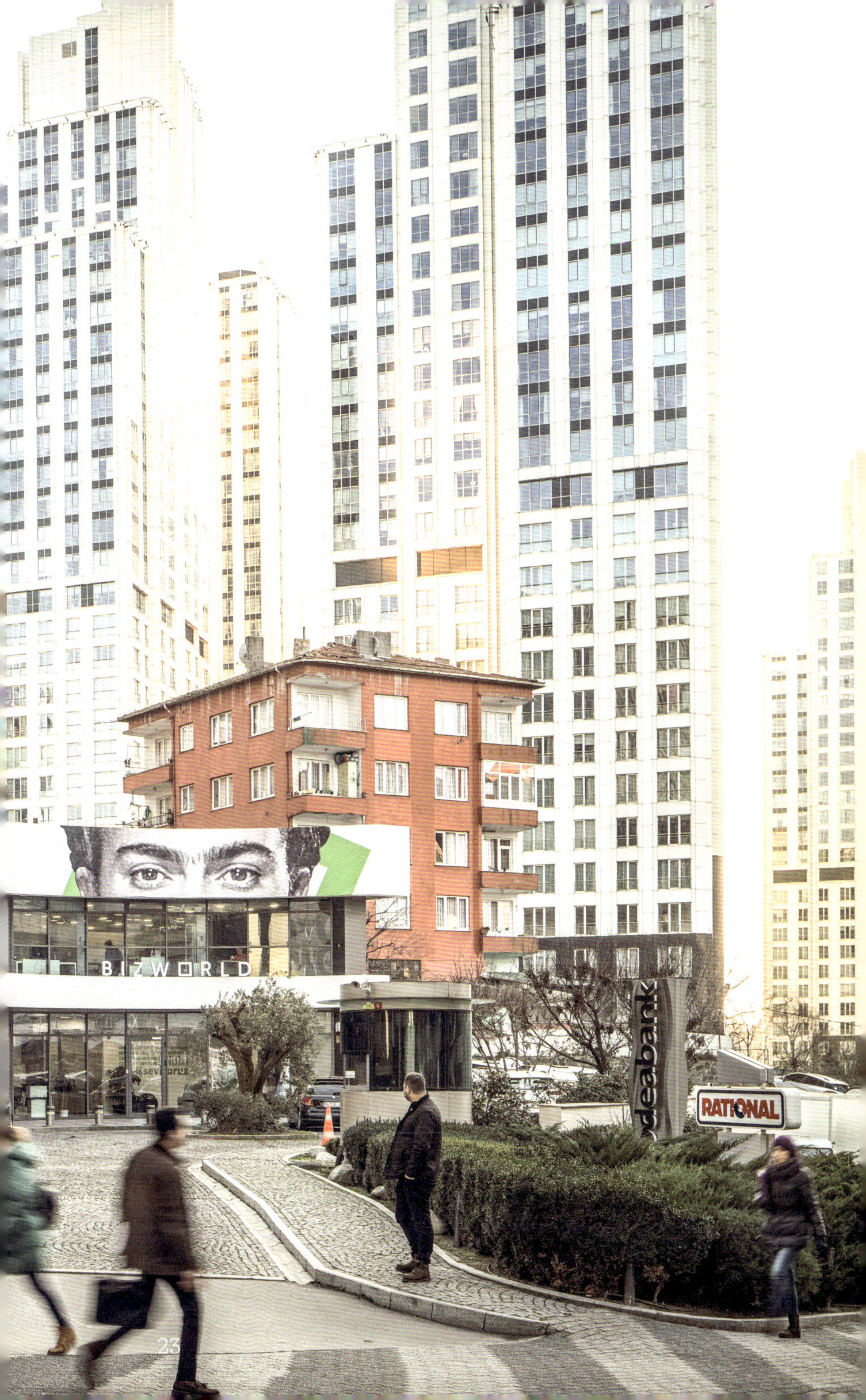
BIZWORLD
RATIONAL

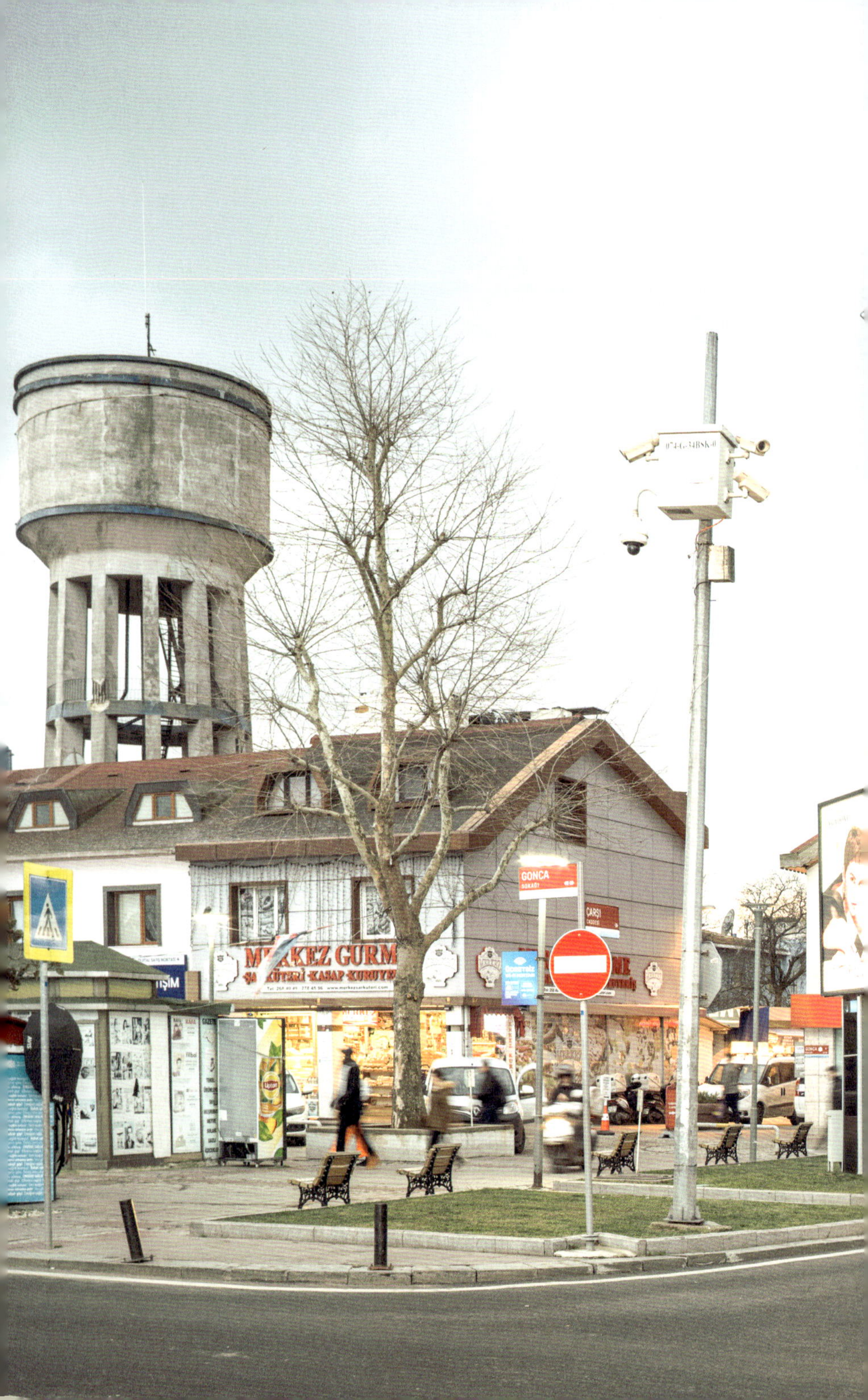
GONCA
ÇARŞI
Lipton

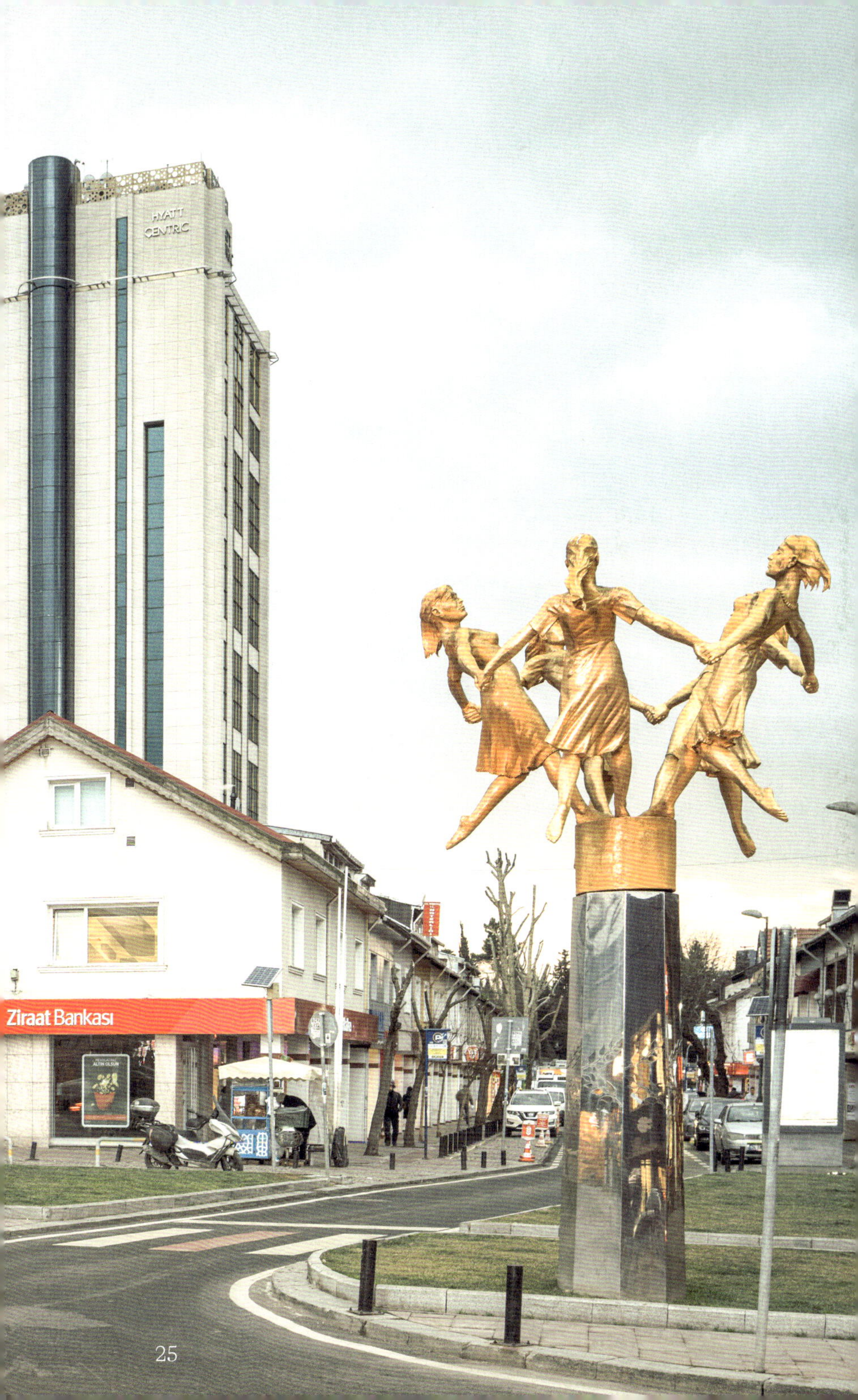
HYATT
CENTRIC
Ziraat Bankası

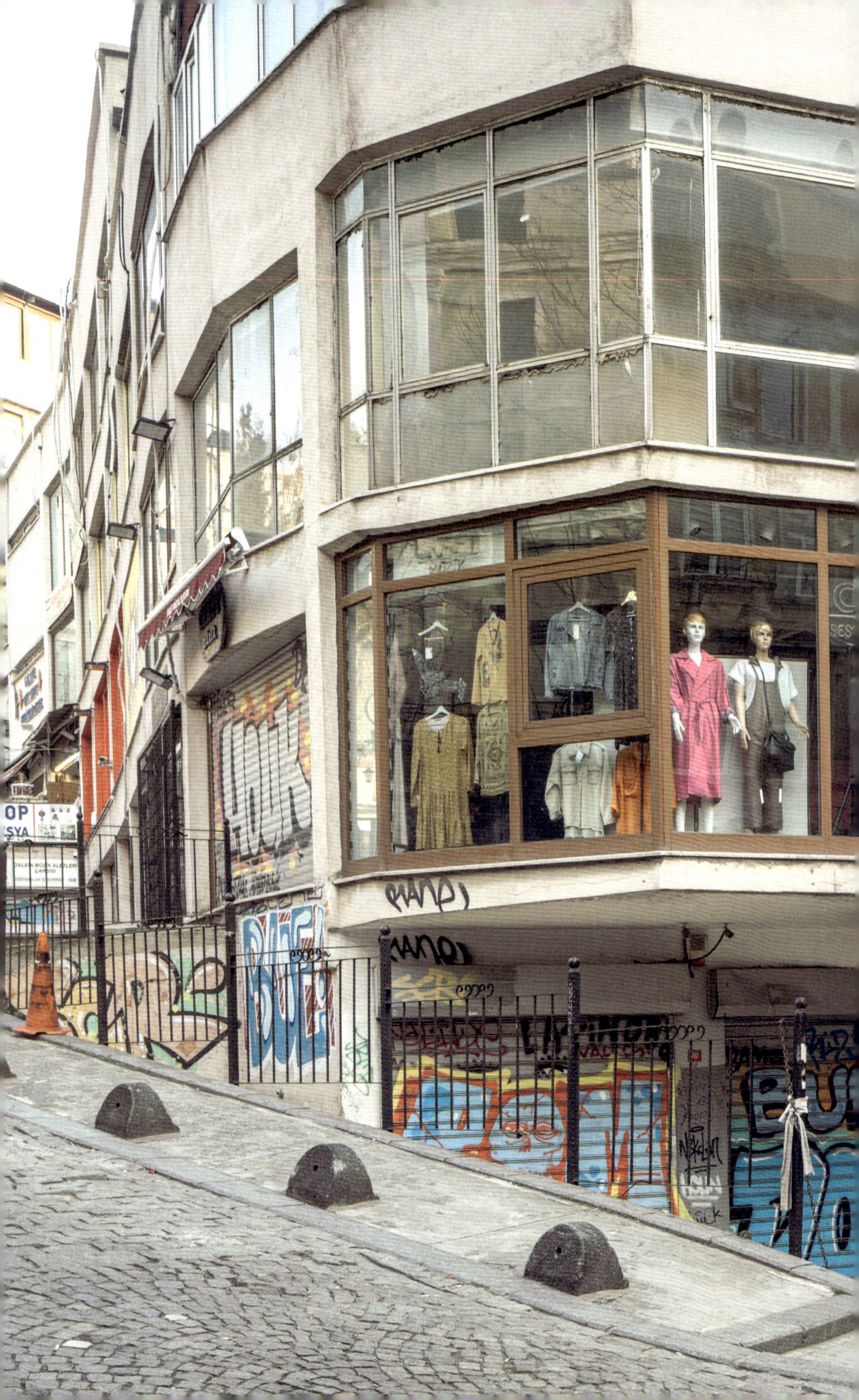

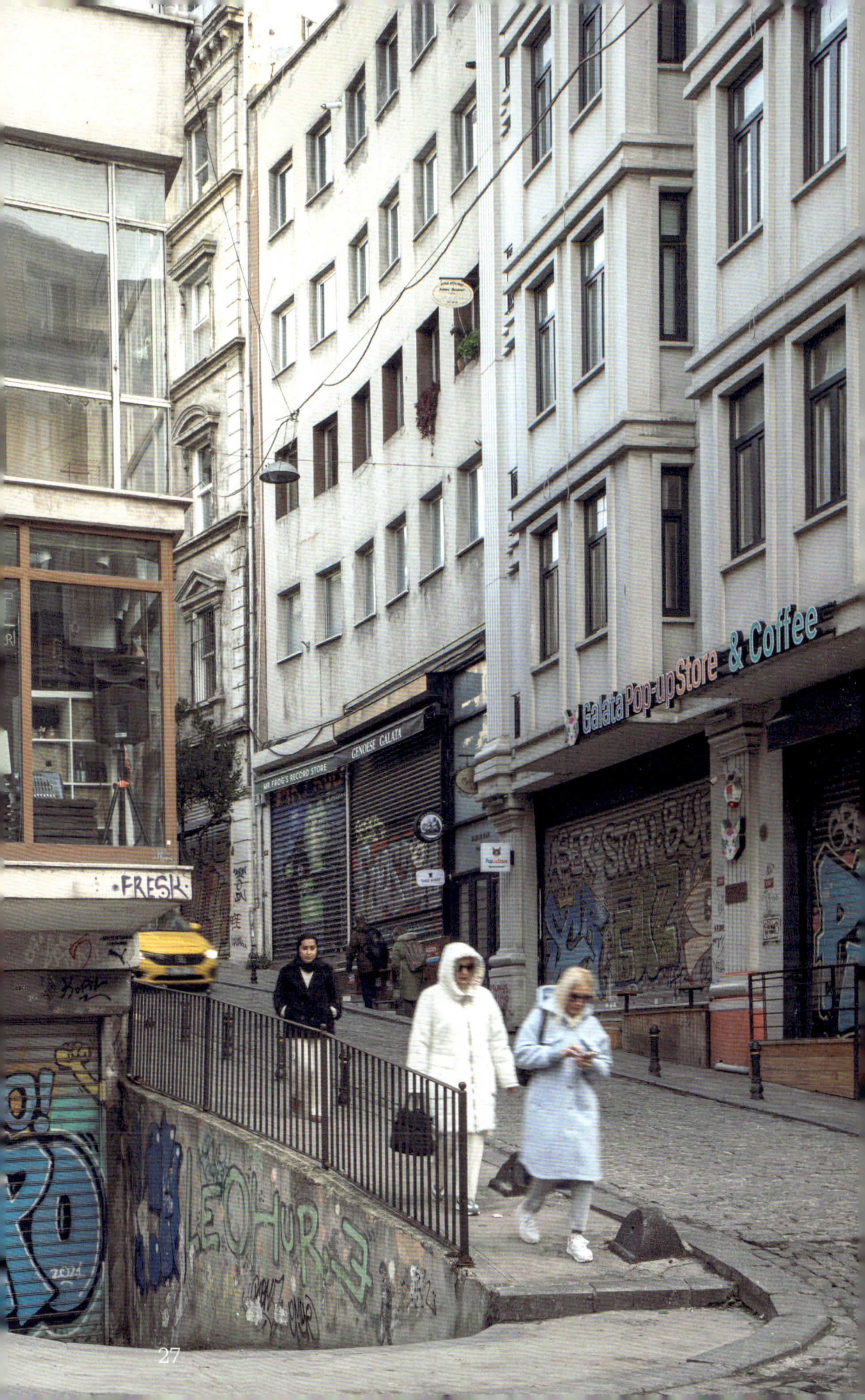
Galata Pop-upStore & Coffee
GENOESE GALATA
MR FROG'S RECORD STORE
FRESK

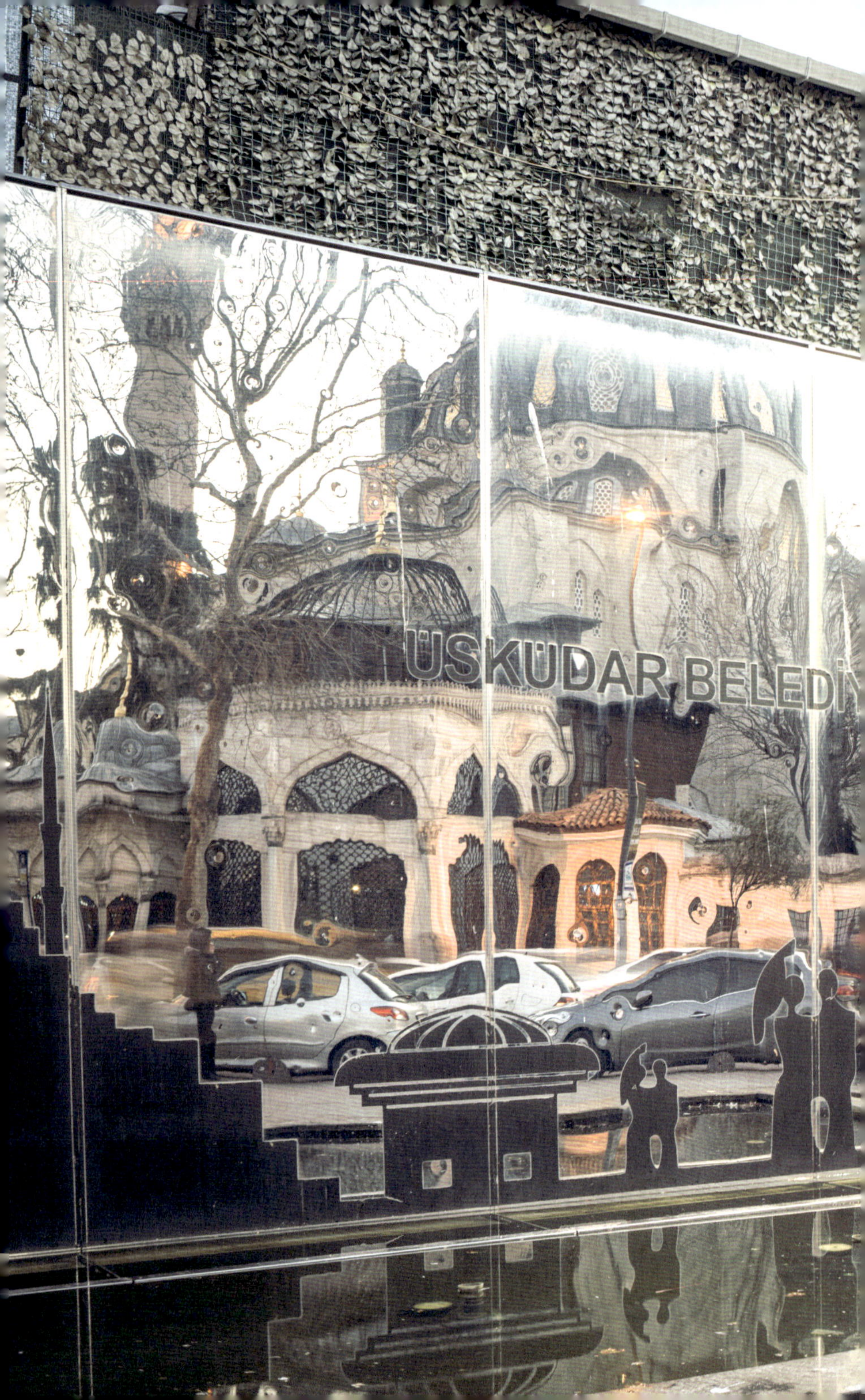
ÜSKÜDAR BELEDİ

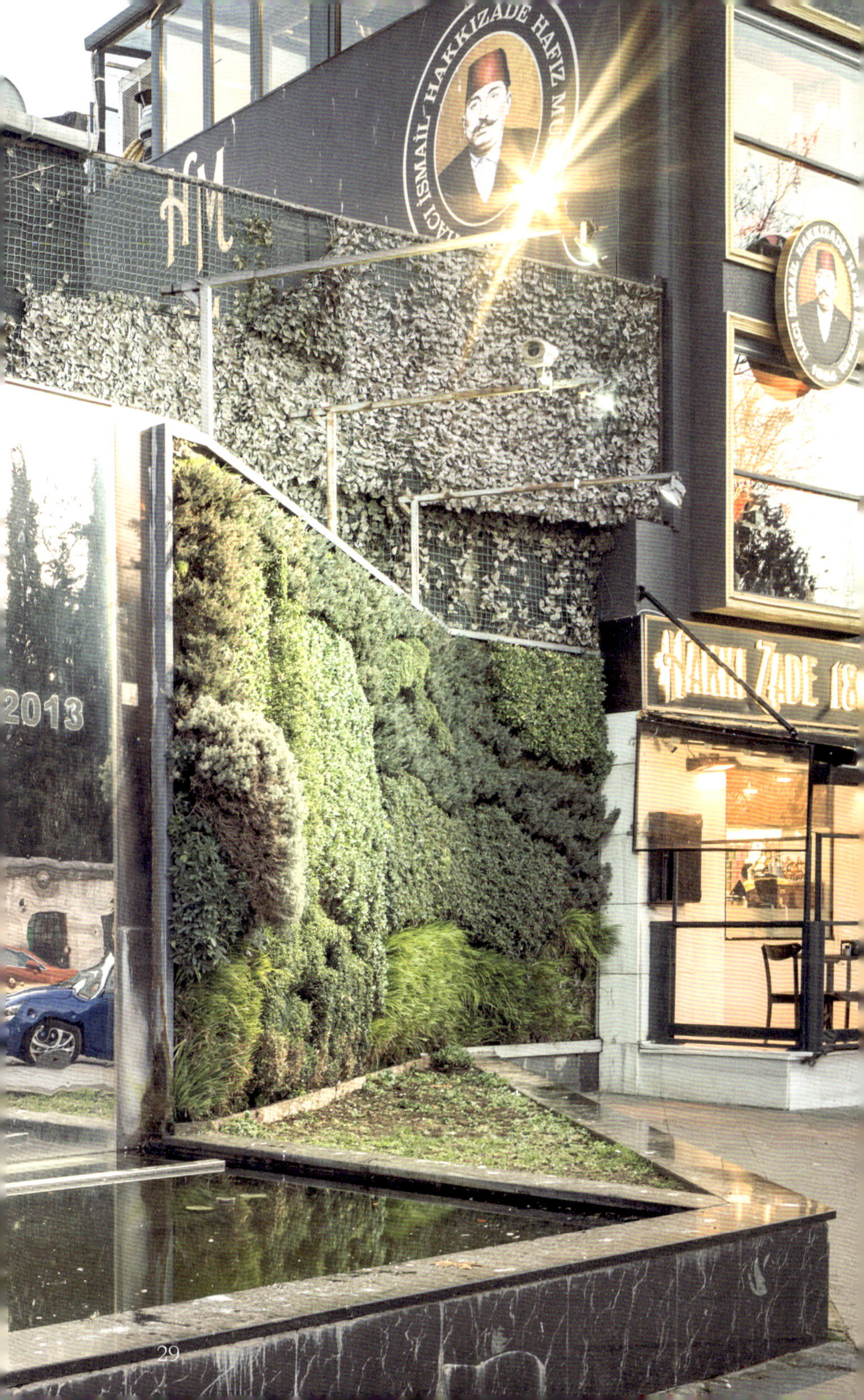
İSMAİL HAKKIZADE HAFIZ
2013
HAKKI ZADE

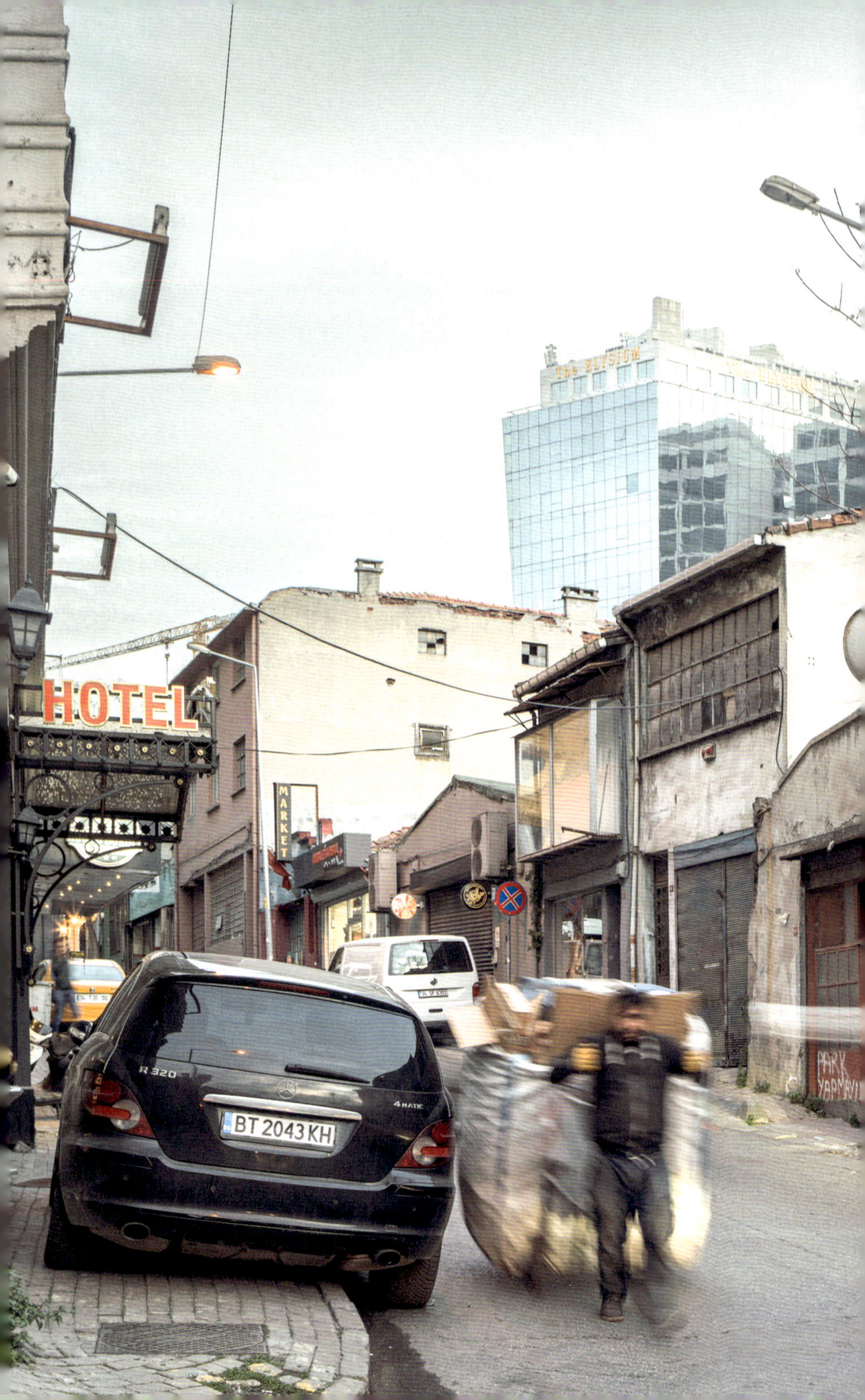
HOTEL
MARKET
The ELYSIUM
R 320
BT 2043 KH
PARK
YAPMAYI

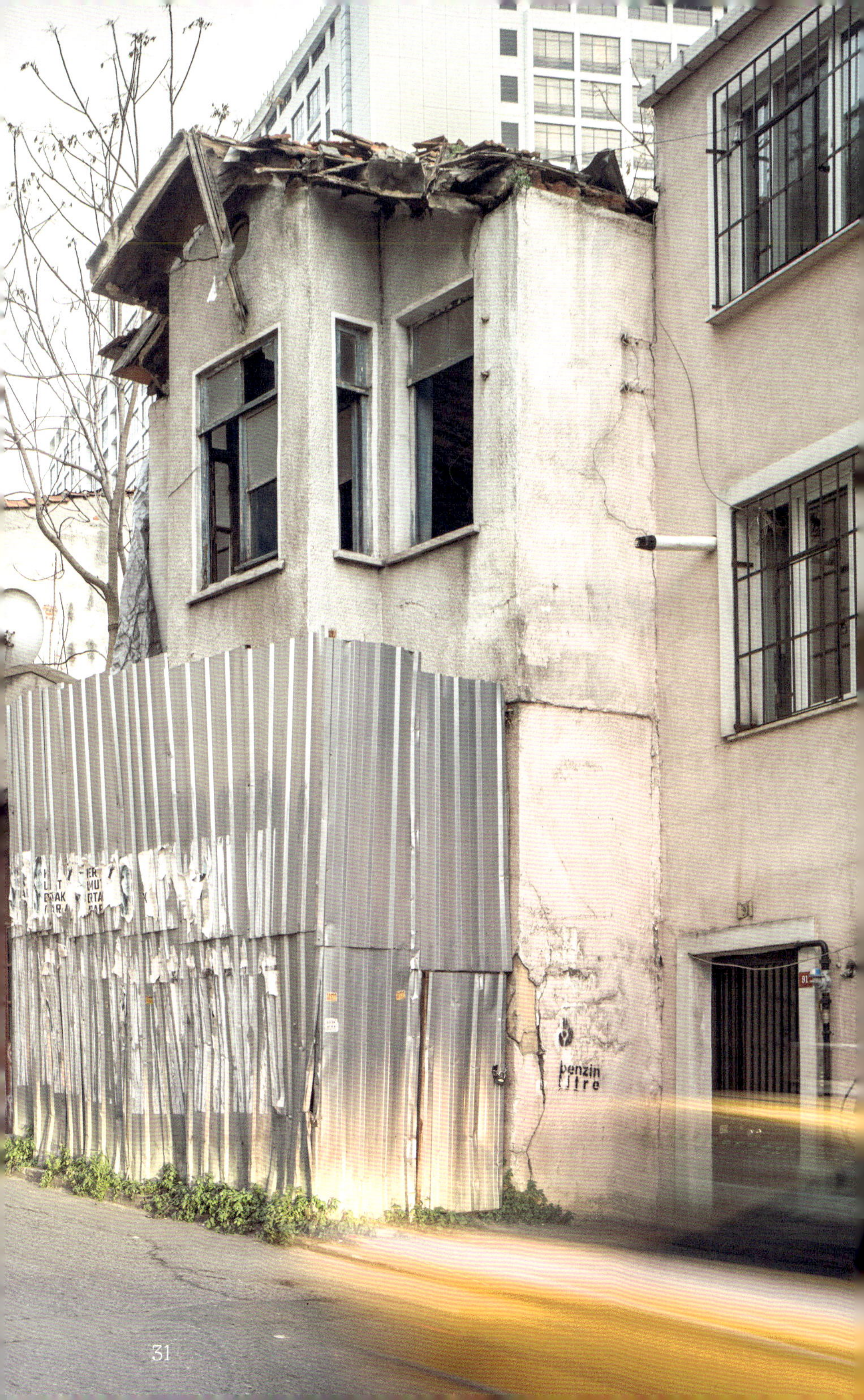
benzin
litre

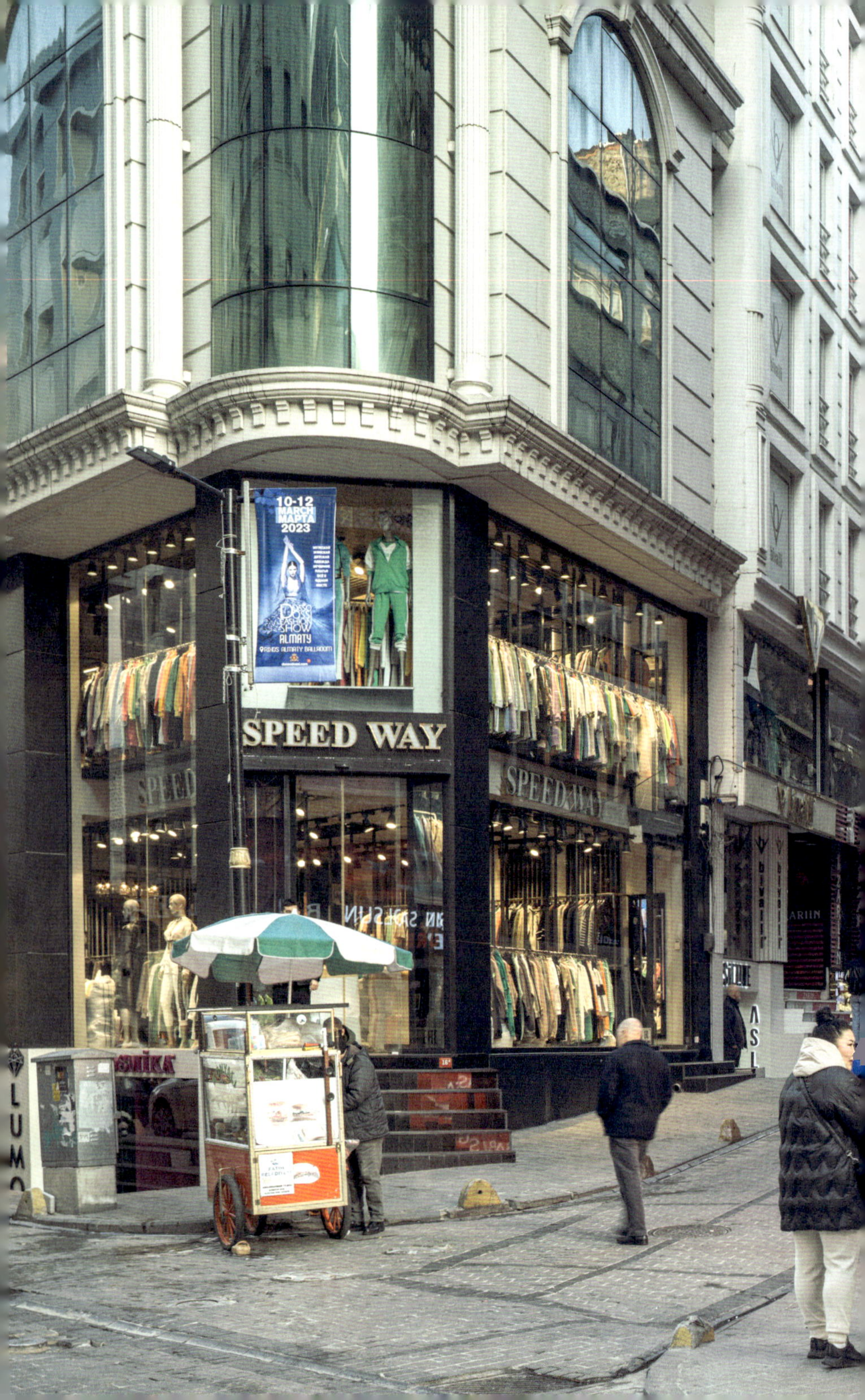
10-12
MARCH
МАРТА
2023
ALMATY
SPEED WAY
SPEEDWAY

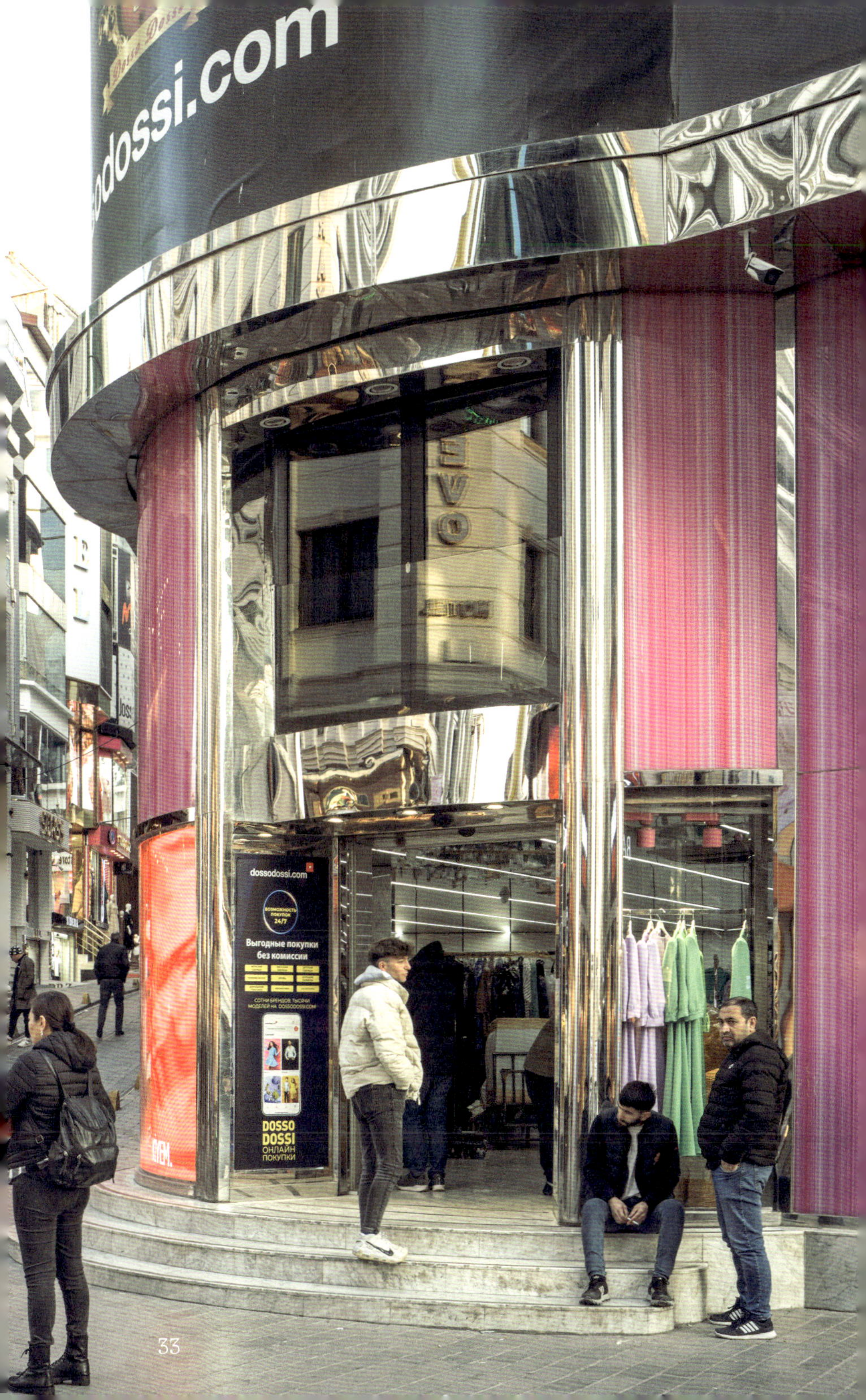
odossi.com
dossodossi.com
ВОЗМОЖНОСТЬ ПОКУПОК 24/7
Выгодные покупки без комиссии
СОТНИ БРЕНДОВ, ТЫСЯЧИ МОДЕЛЕЙ НА DOSSODOSSI.COM
DOSSO DOSSI ОНЛАЙН ПОКУПКИ

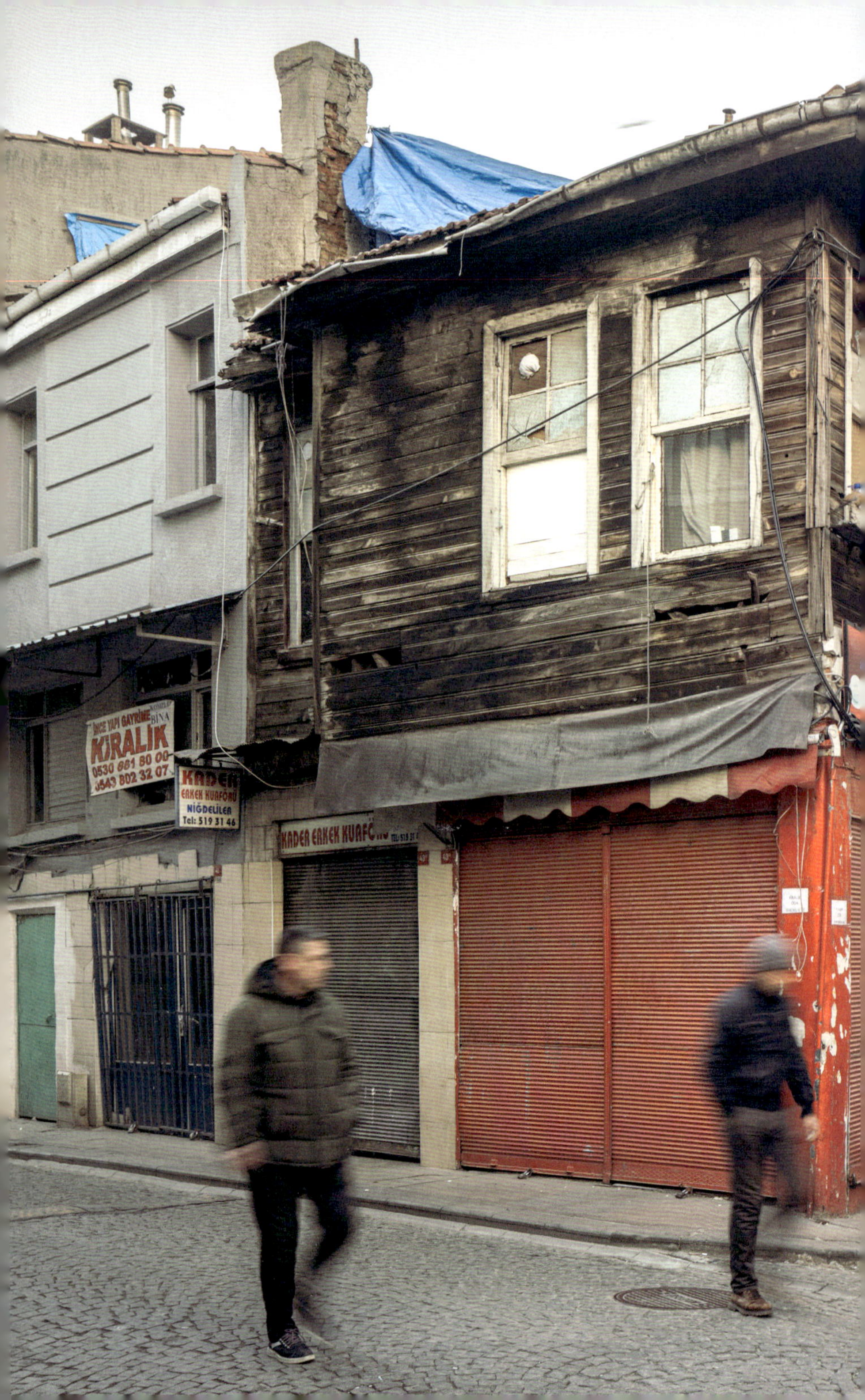
İNCE YAPI GAYRİME
KOMPLE BİNA
KİRALIK
0530 681 80 00
0543 802 32 07
KADER
ERKEK KUAFÖRÜ
NİĞDELİLER
Tel: 519 31 46
KADER ERKEK

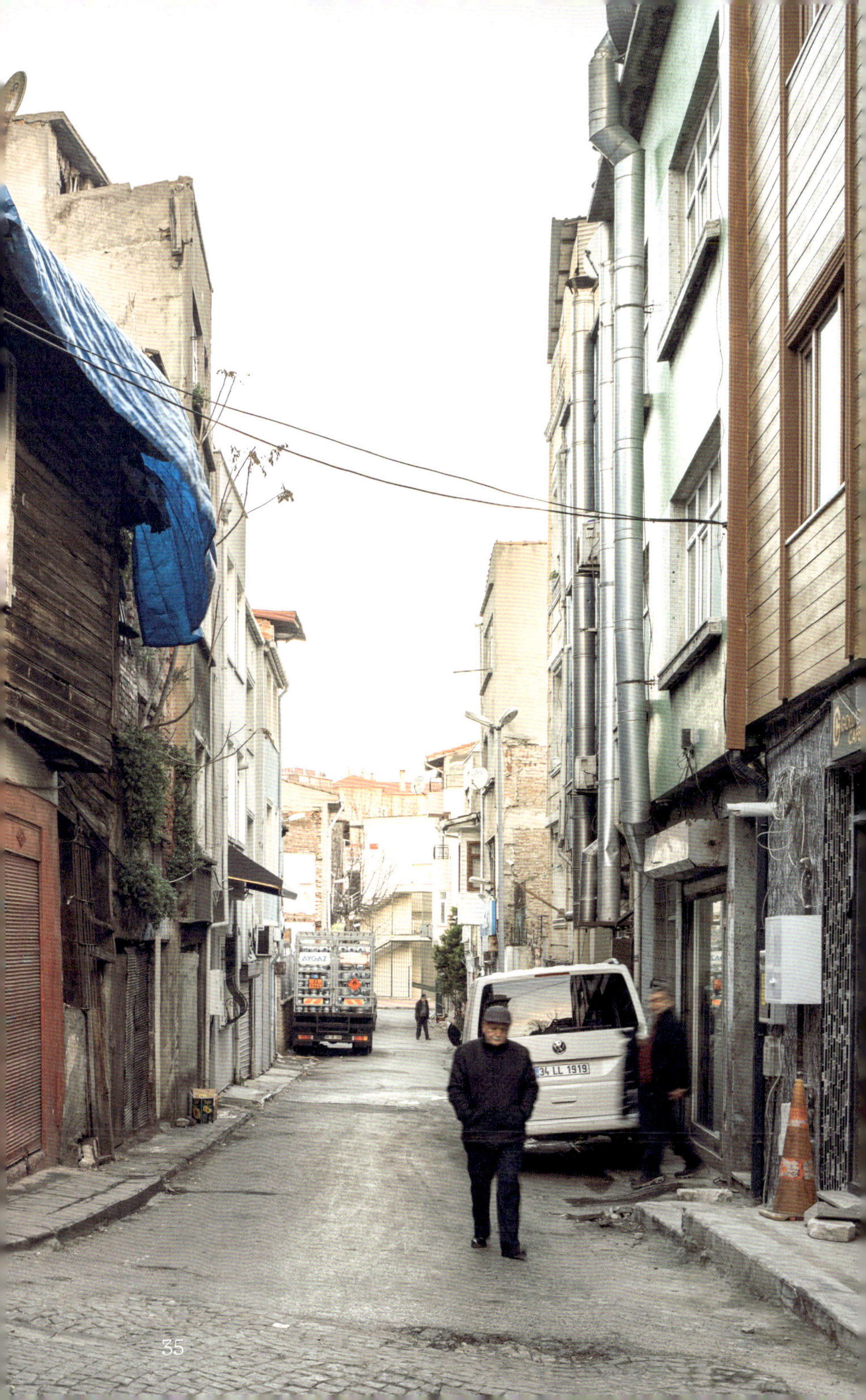
AYGAZ
34 LL 1919

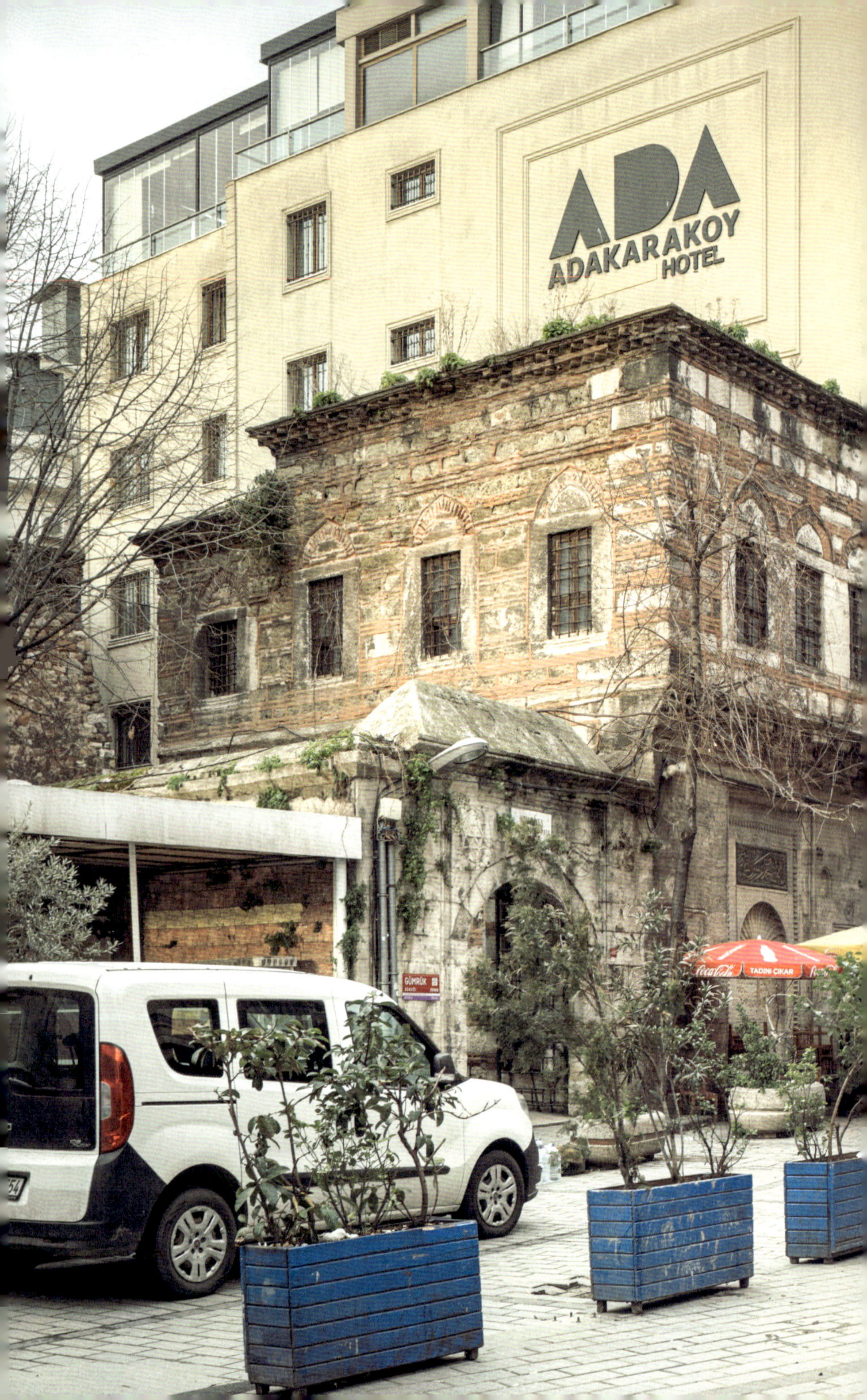
ADA
ADAKARAKOY
HOTEL
GÜMRÜK
Coca-Cola
TADINI ÇIKAR

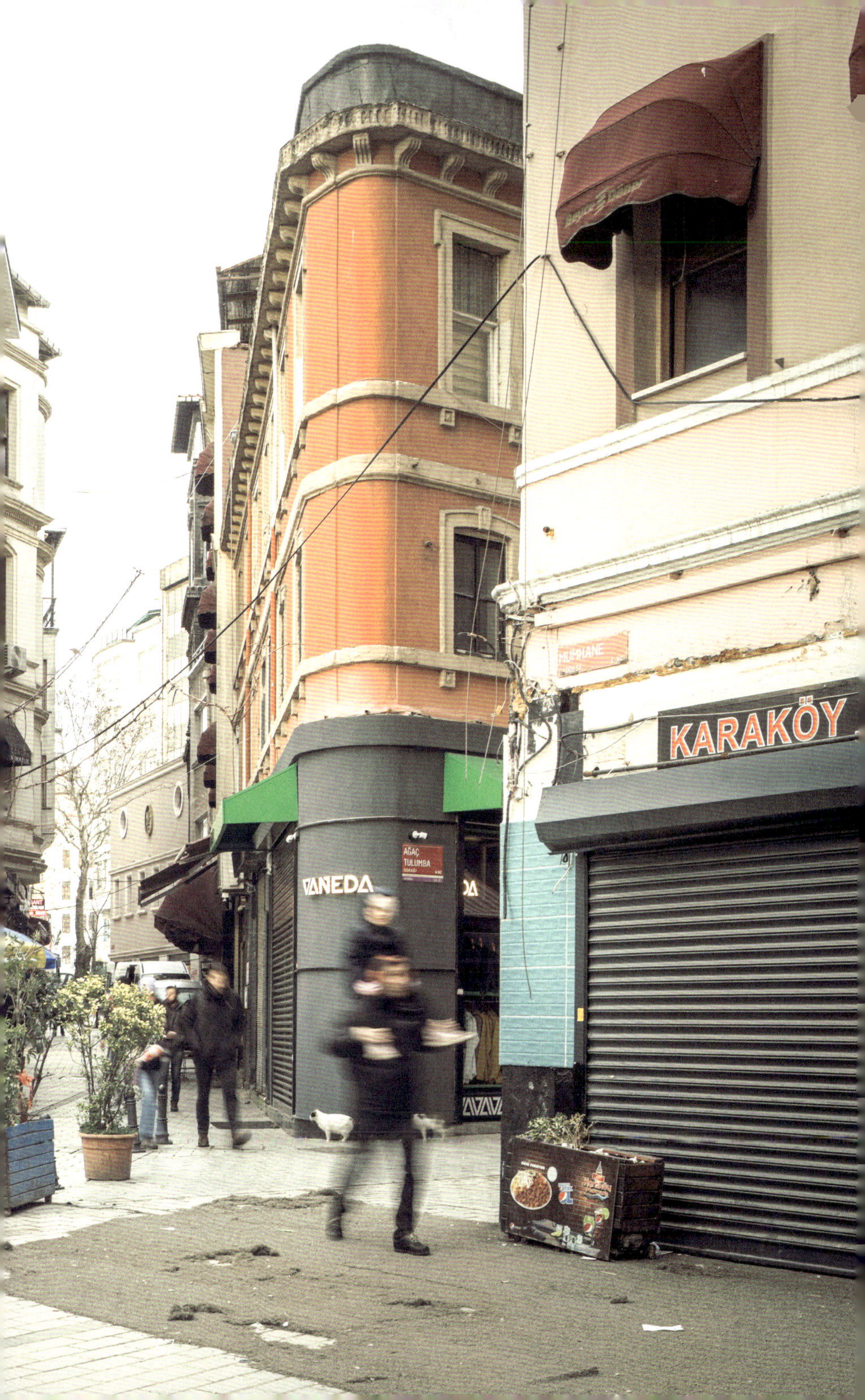

MUMHANE
KARAKÖY
AĞAÇ
TULUMBA

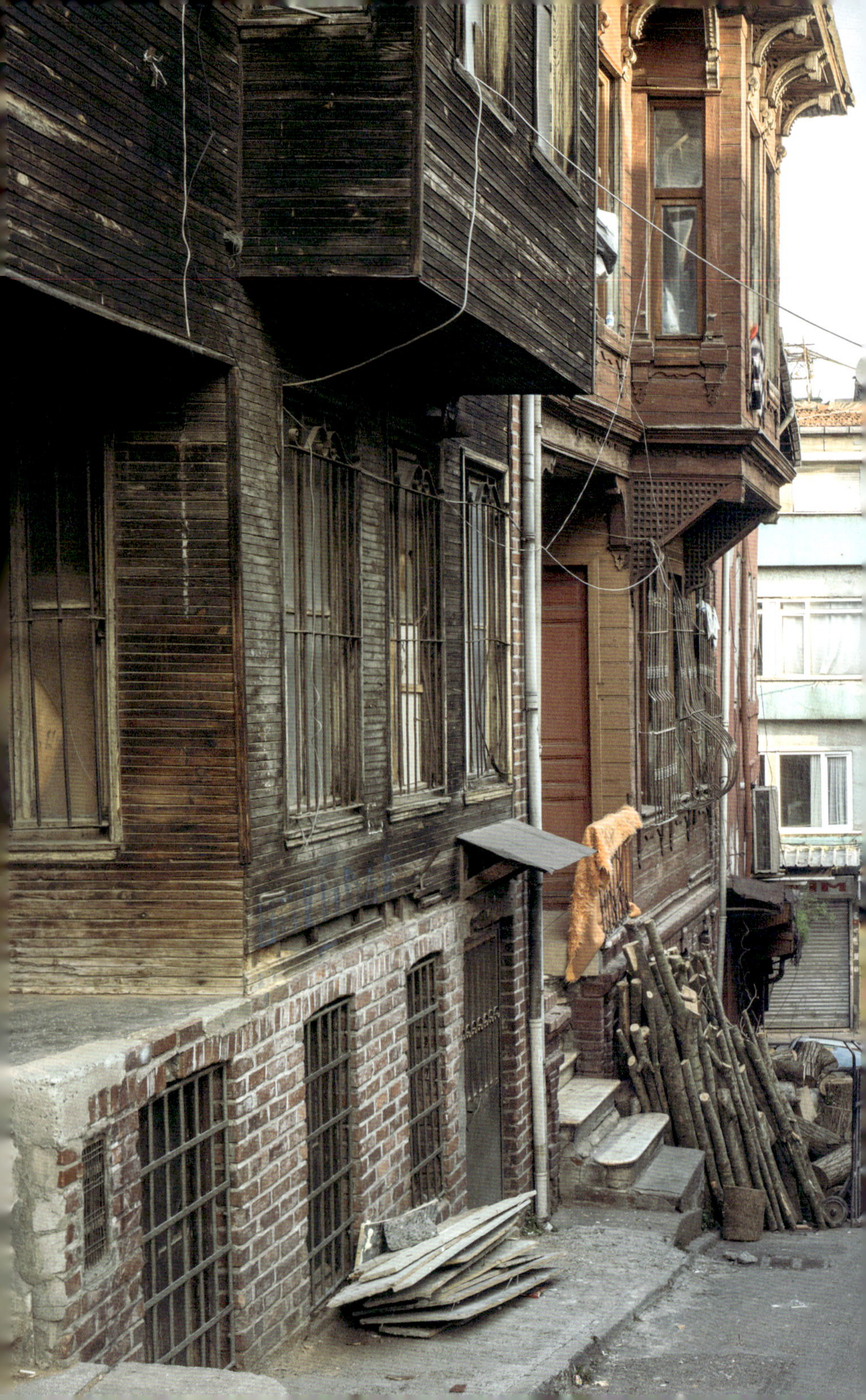

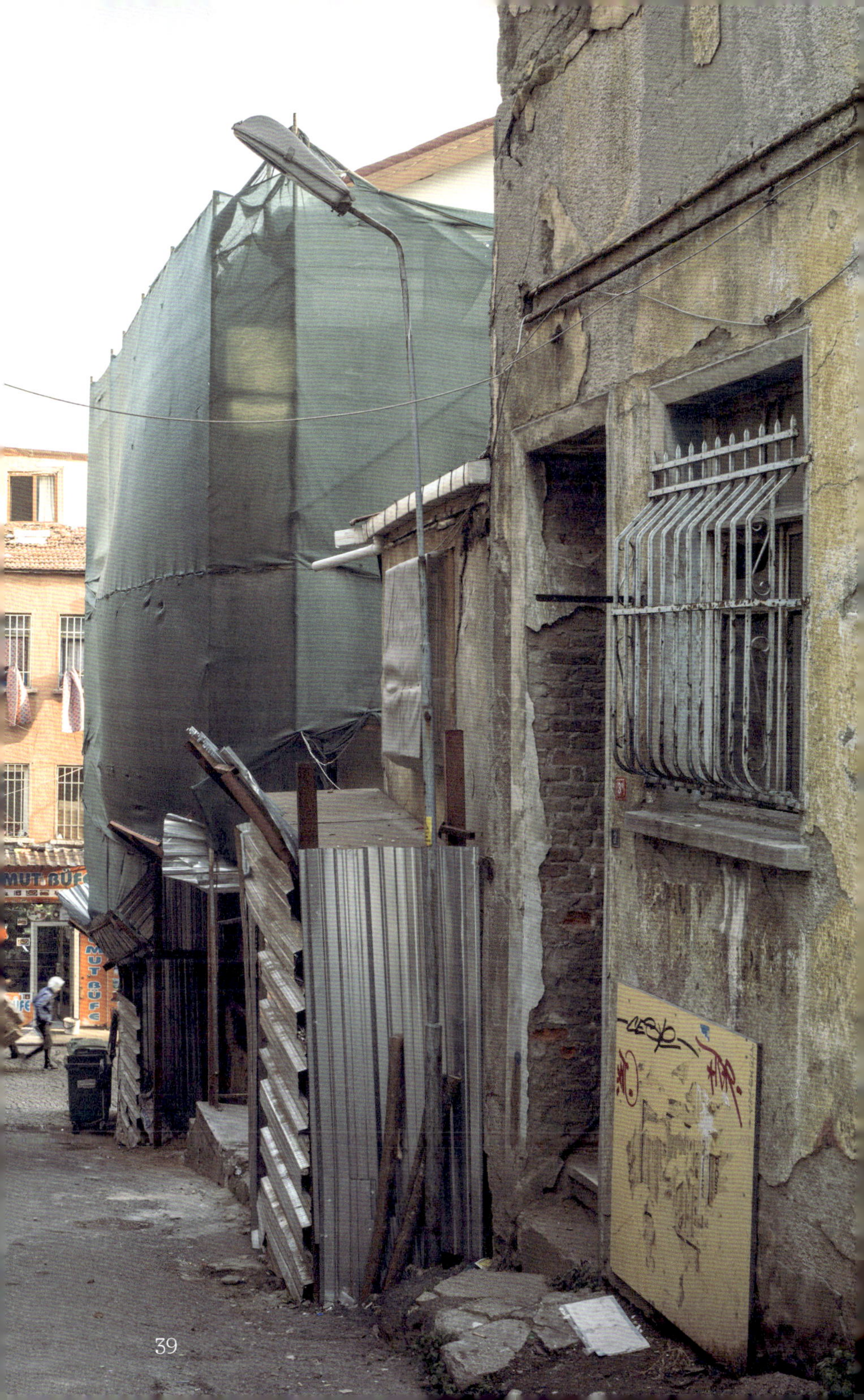

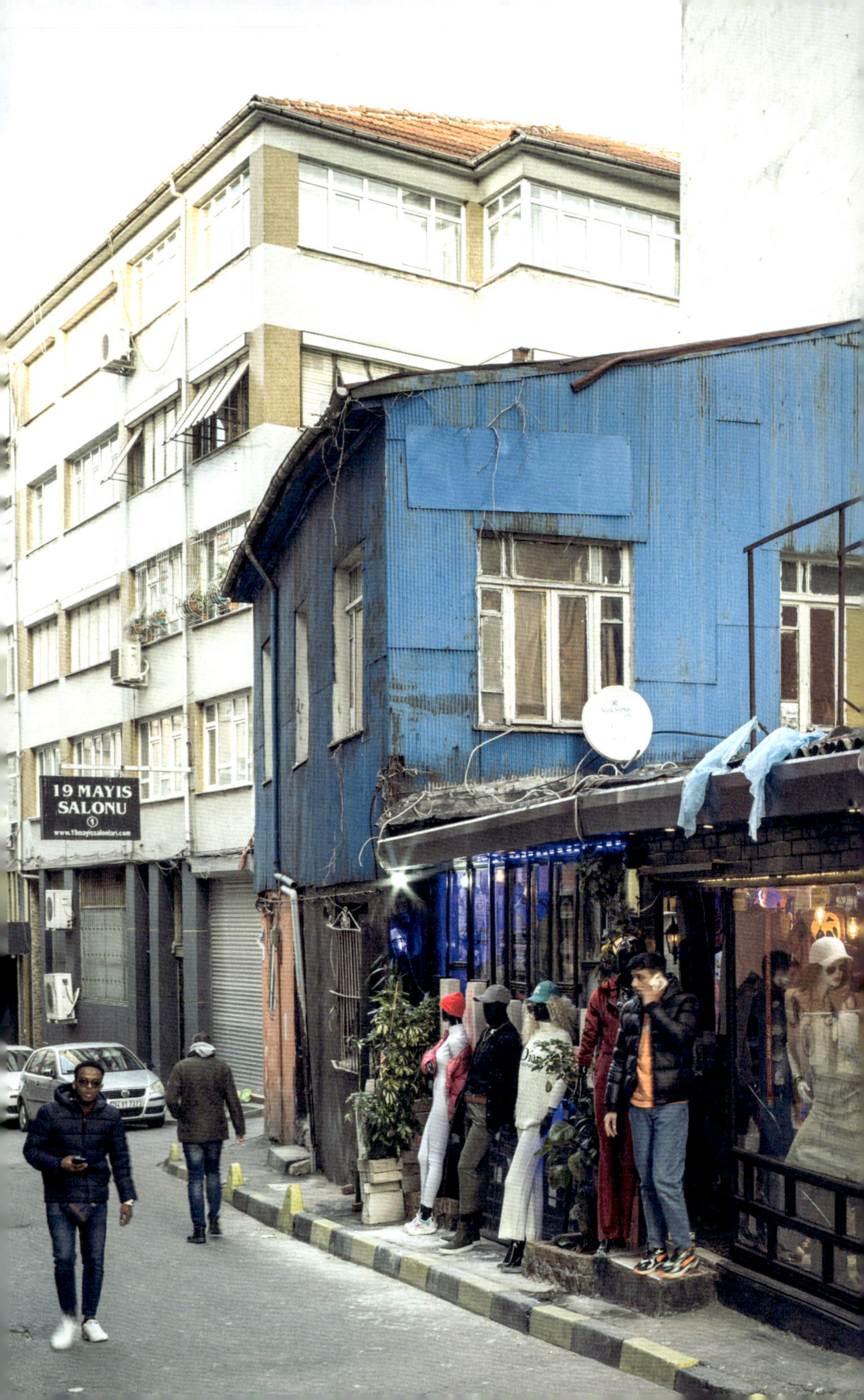
19 MAYIS
SALONU
1
www.19mayissalonlari.com

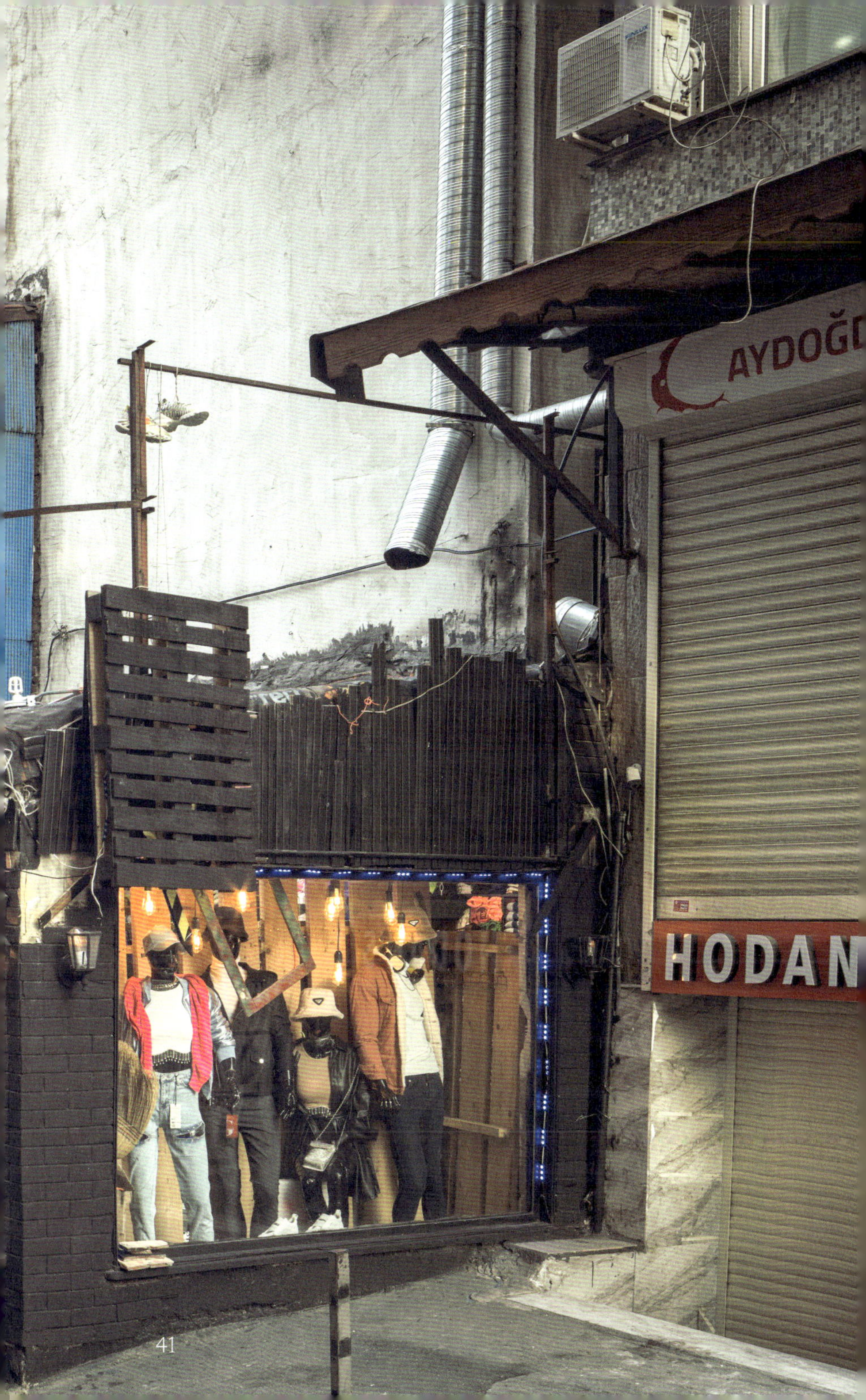
AYDOĞD
HODAN

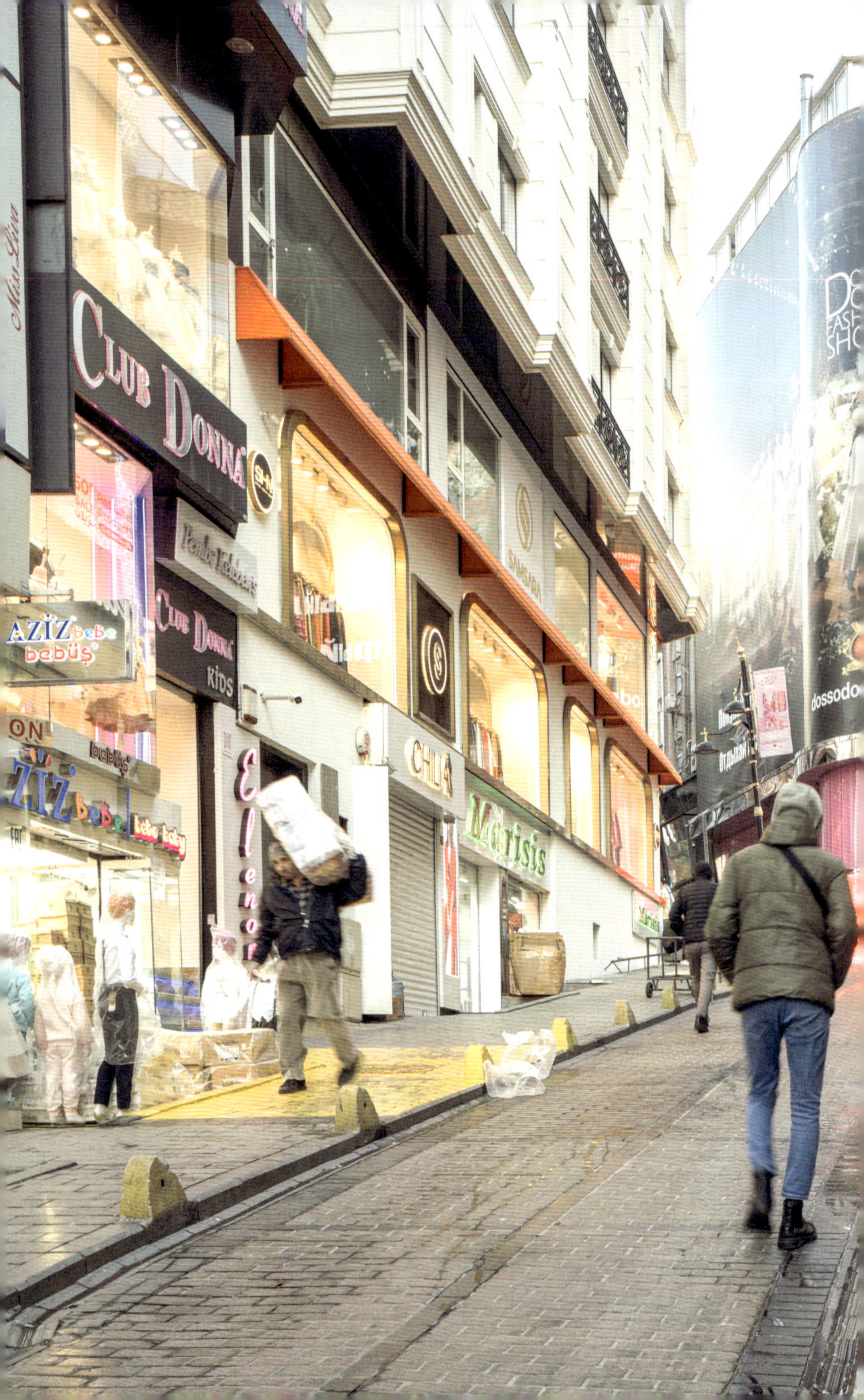
CLUB DONNA
AZİZ bebe
bebüş
CLUB DONNA
KIDS
AZİZ bebe
bebüş
Marisis
dossodo

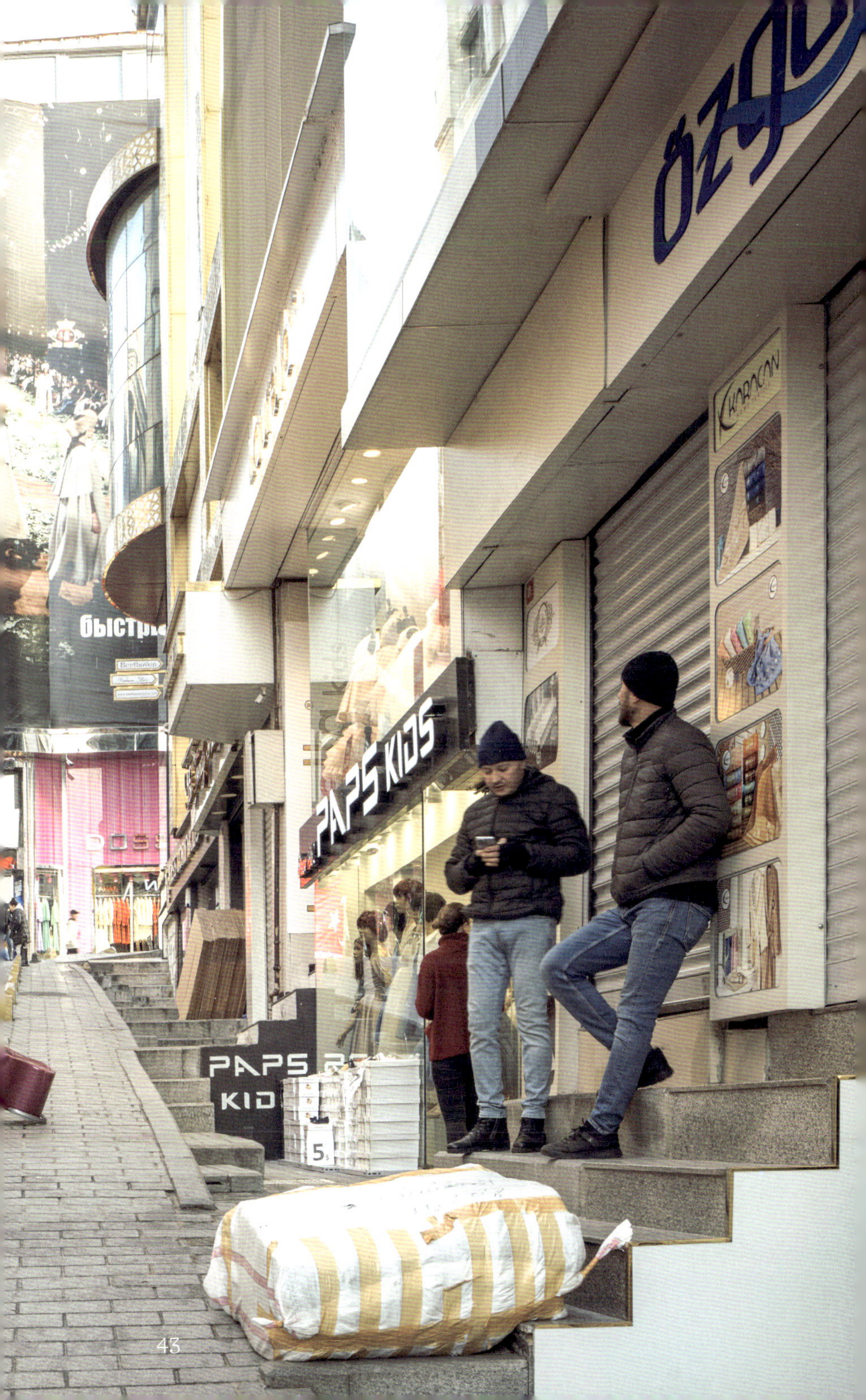
PAPS KIDS
Beethoven

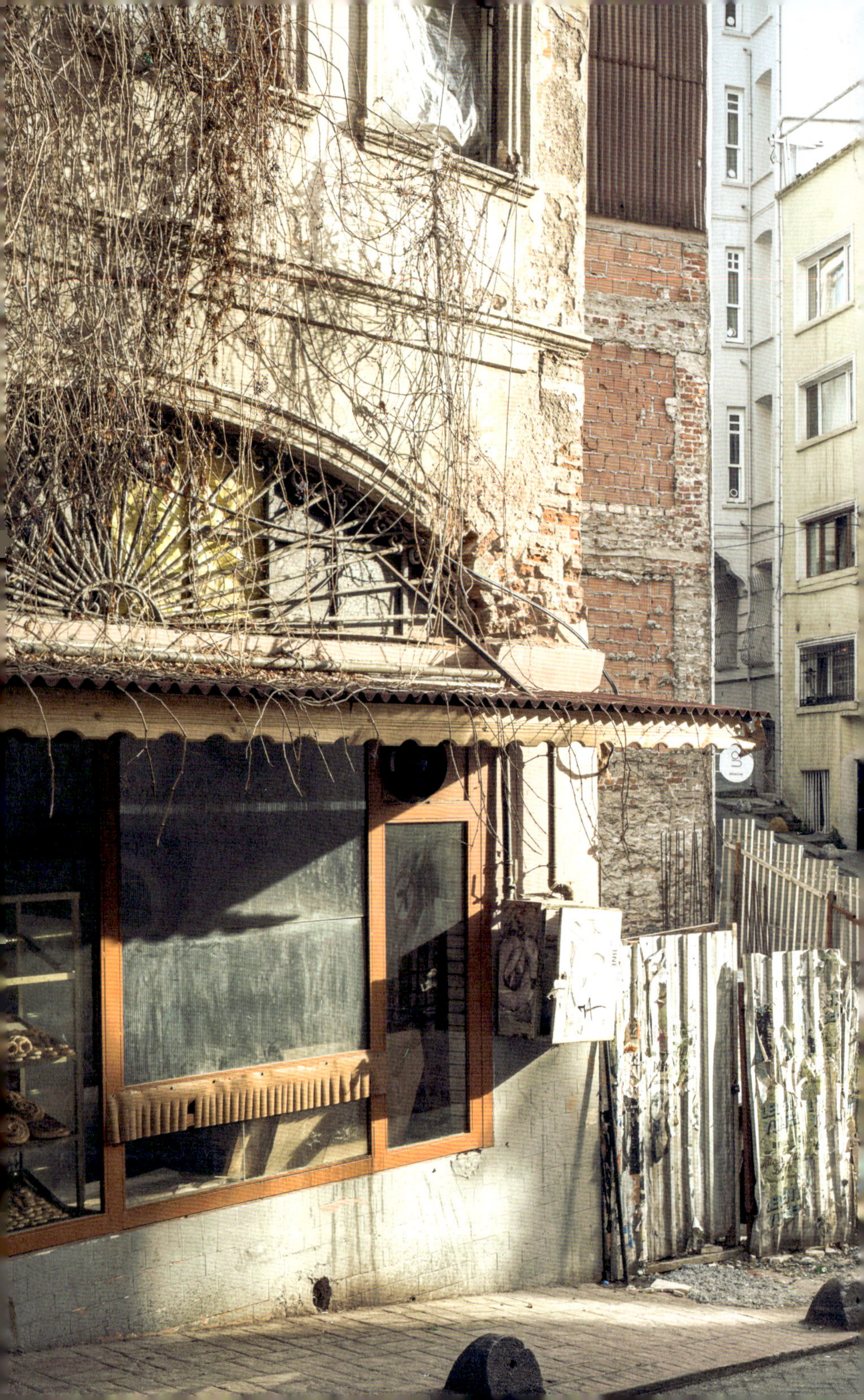

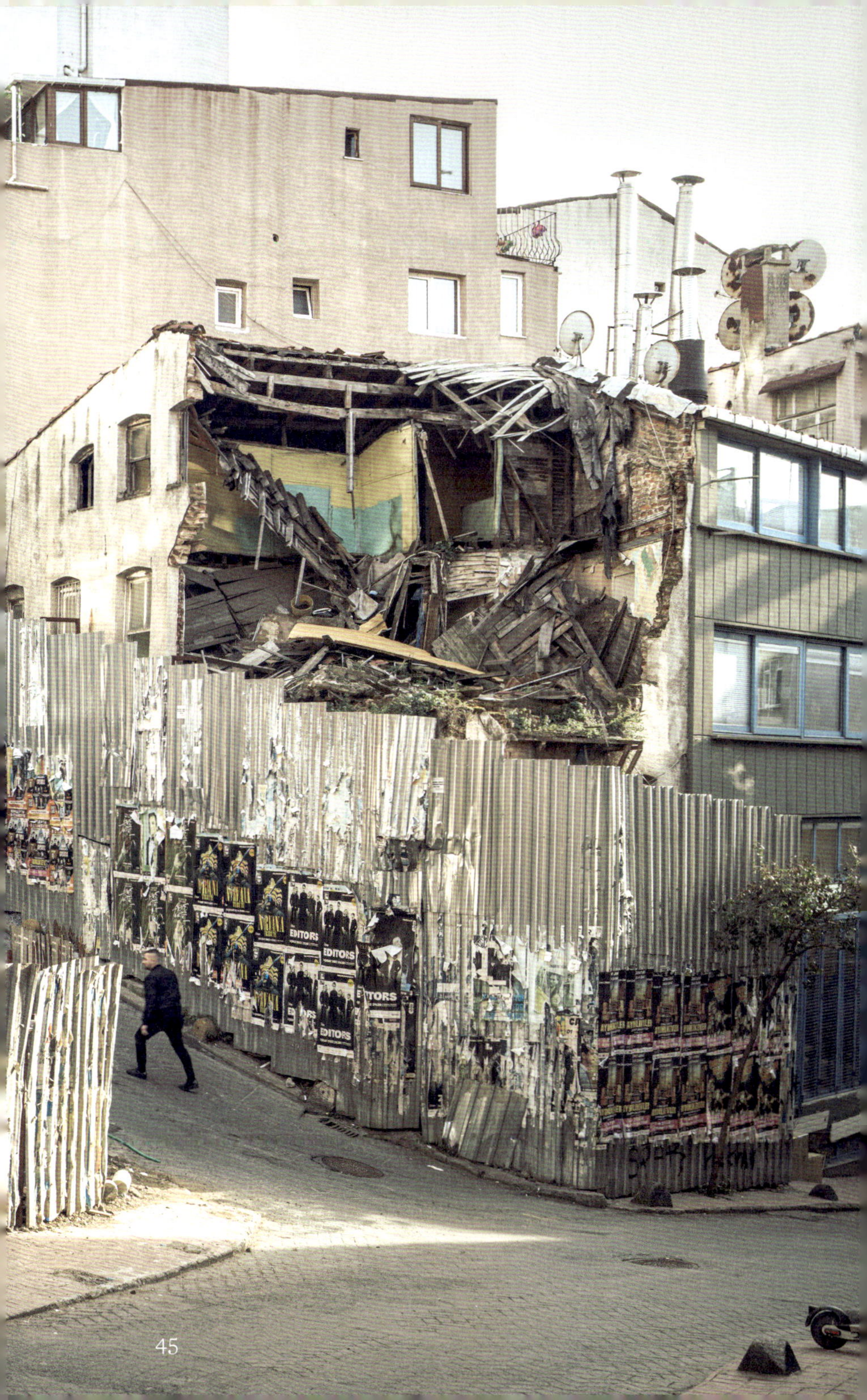
EDITORS

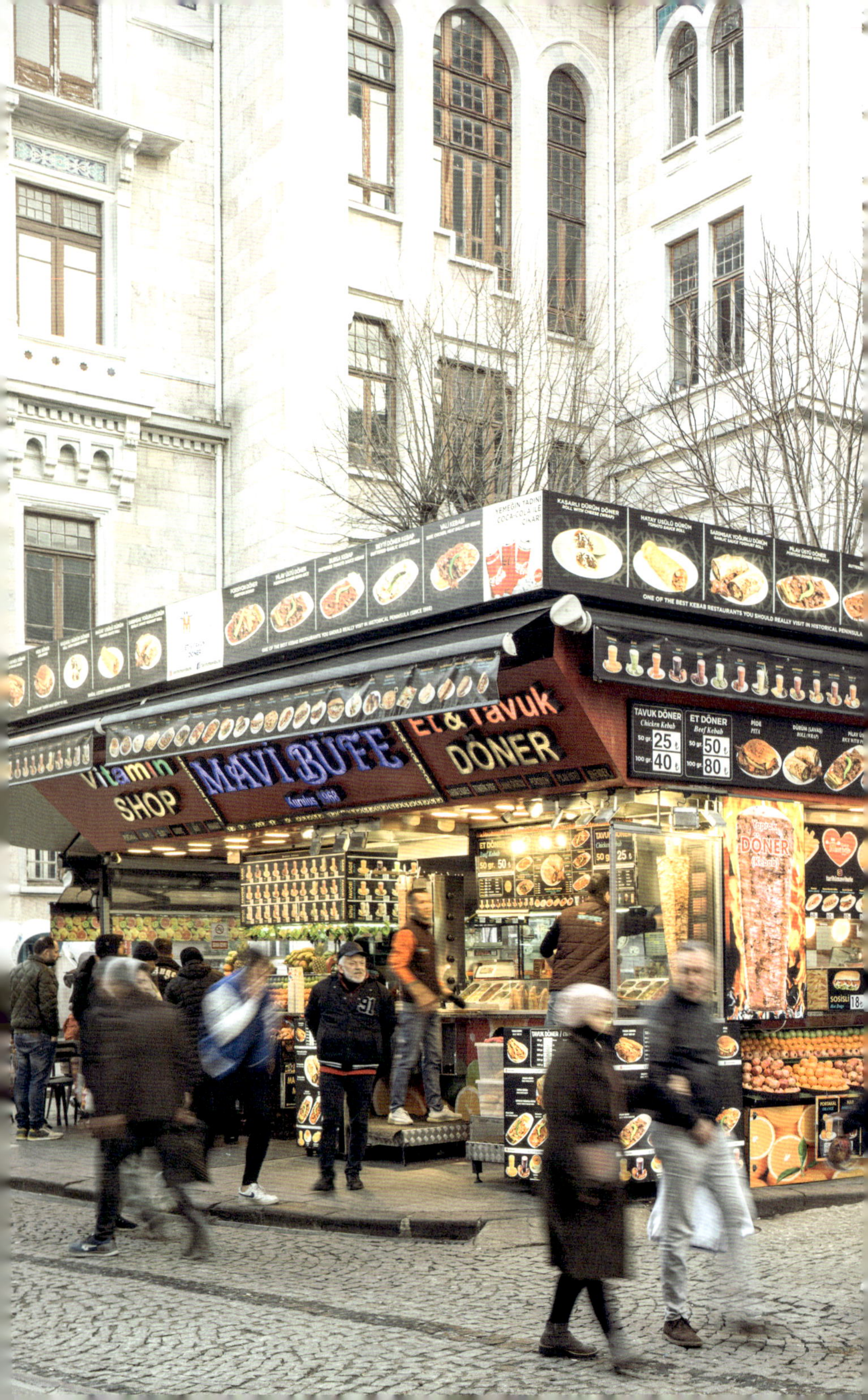

Vitamin
SHOP
MAVI BÜFE
Et & Tavuk
DÖNER
TAVUK DÖNER
Chicken Kebab
50 gr. 25
100 gr. 40
ET DÖNER
Beef Kebab
50 gr. 50
100 gr. 80
PİDE
KAŞARLI DÜRÜM DÖNER
HATAY USÜLÜ DÜRÜM
ONE OF THE BEST KEBAB RESTAURANTS YOU SHOULD REALLY VISIT IN HISTORICAL PENINSULA
DÖNER

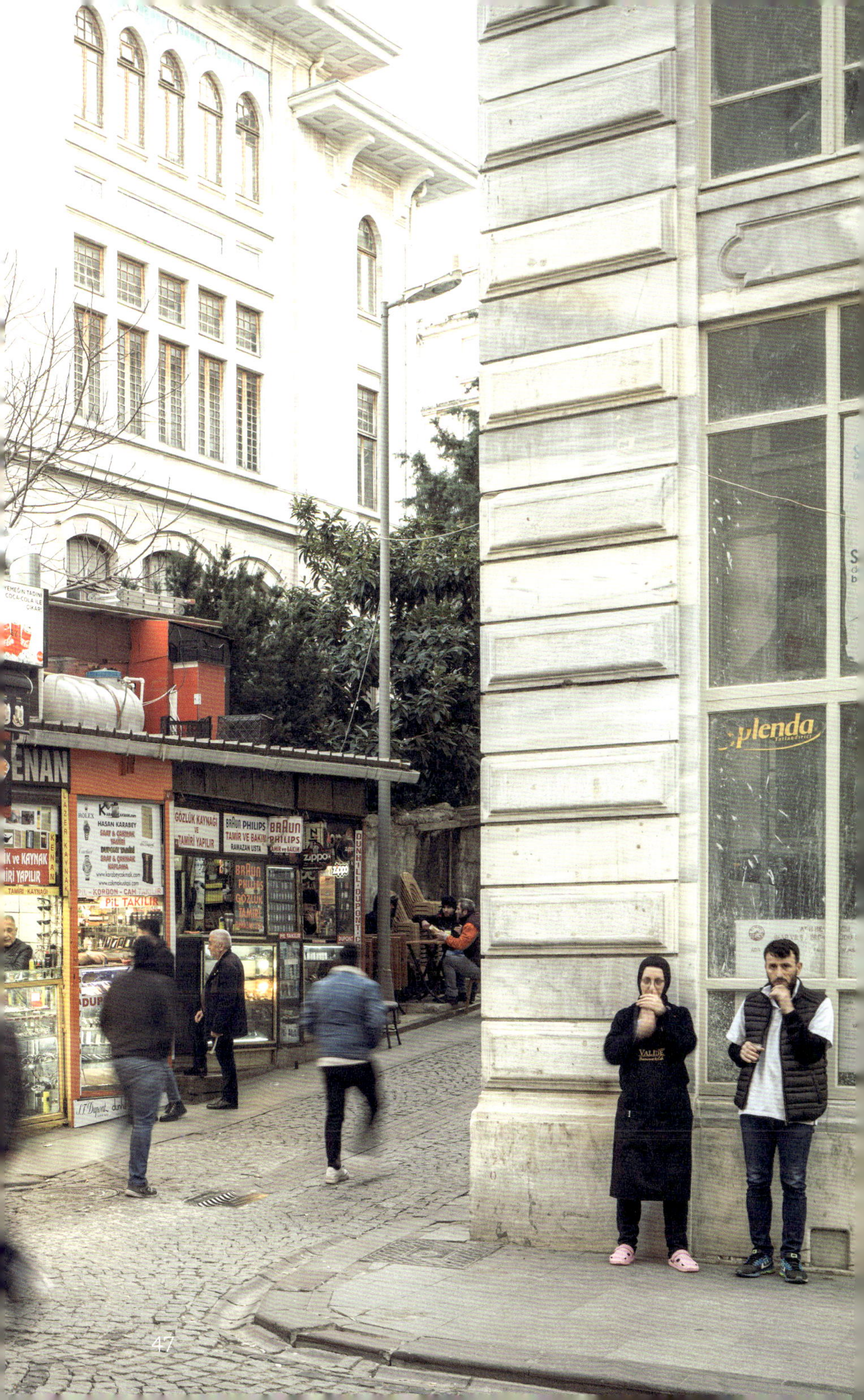
ENAN
LAZER KAYNAK
KENAN
IK ve KAYNAK
IRI YAPILIR
TAMIRI KAYNAĞI
ROLEX
HASAN KARABEY
Cartier
www.karabeycakmak.com
www.cakmakustasi.com
PİL TAKILIR
GÖZLÜK KAYNAĞI
VE
TAMİRİ YAPILIR
BRAUN PHILIPS
TAMIR VE BAKIM
RAMAZAN USTA
BRAUN
PHILIPS
TAMIR ve BAKIM
ZIPPO
ZIPPO
DUNHILL.DUPONT.C
DUPONT
PİL TAKILIR
VALIDE
plenda

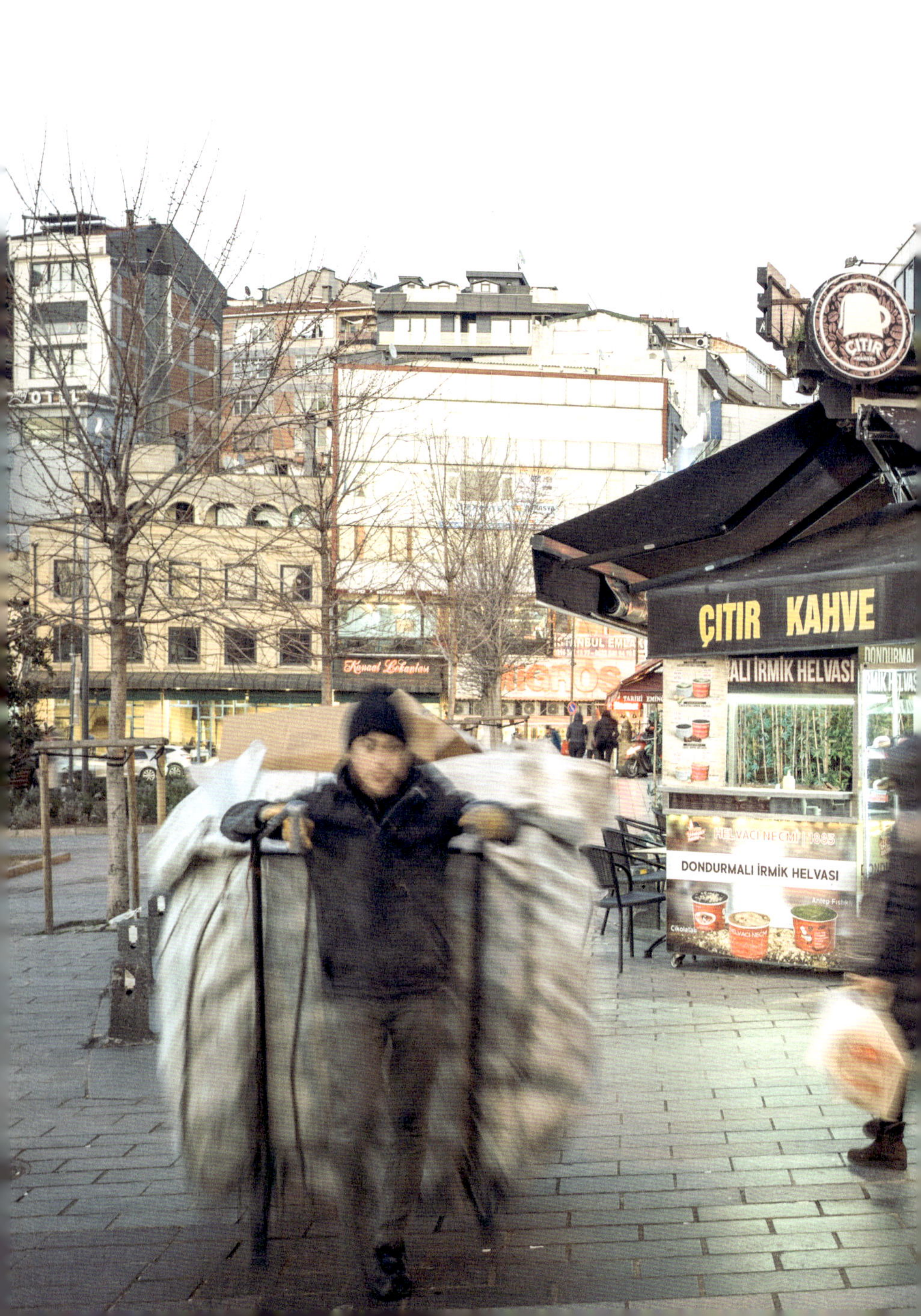
ÇITIR KAHVE
DONDURMALI İRMİK HELVASI

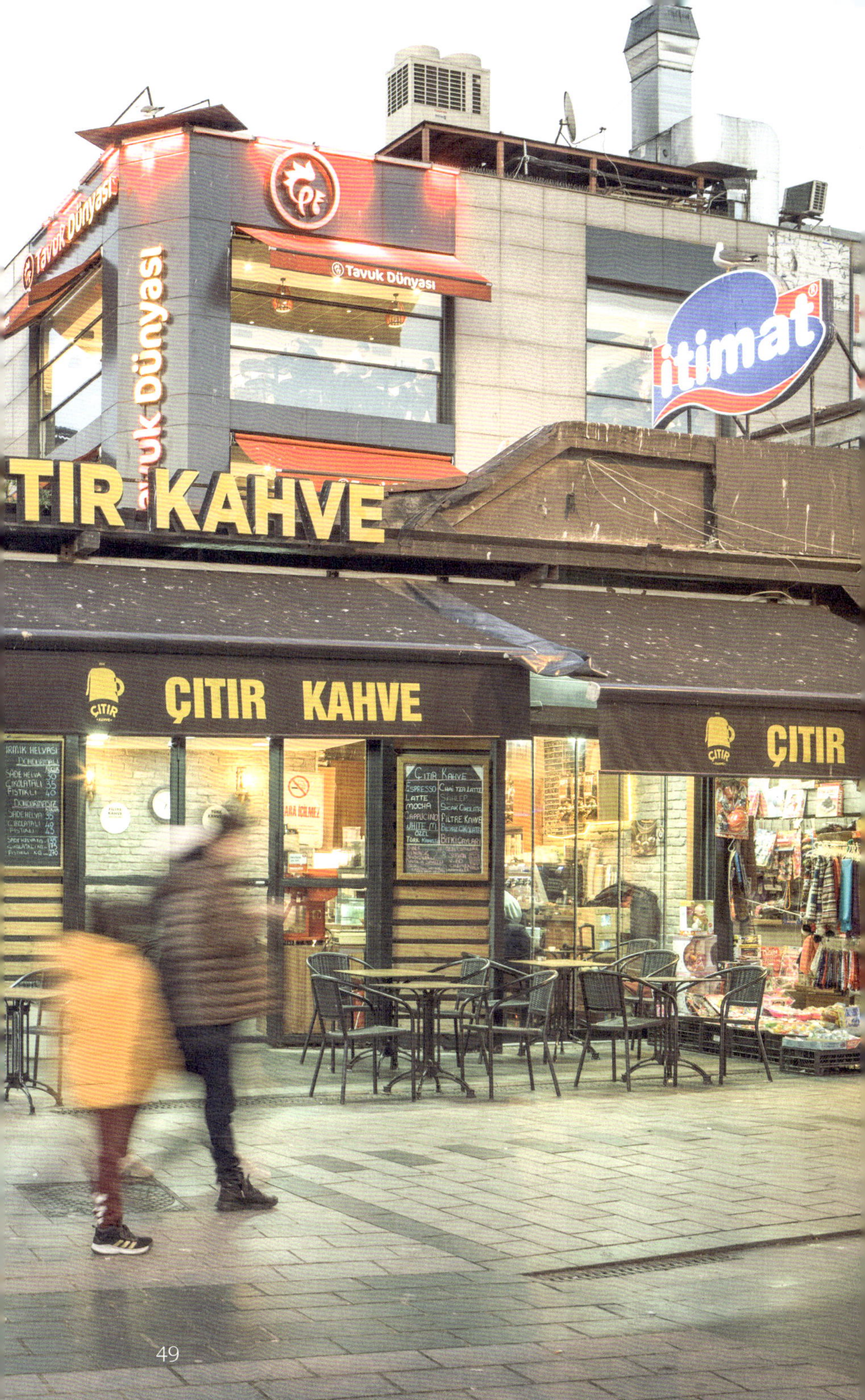

Tavuk Dünyası
Tavuk Dünyası
itimat
TIR KAHVE
ÇITIR KAHVE
ÇITIR

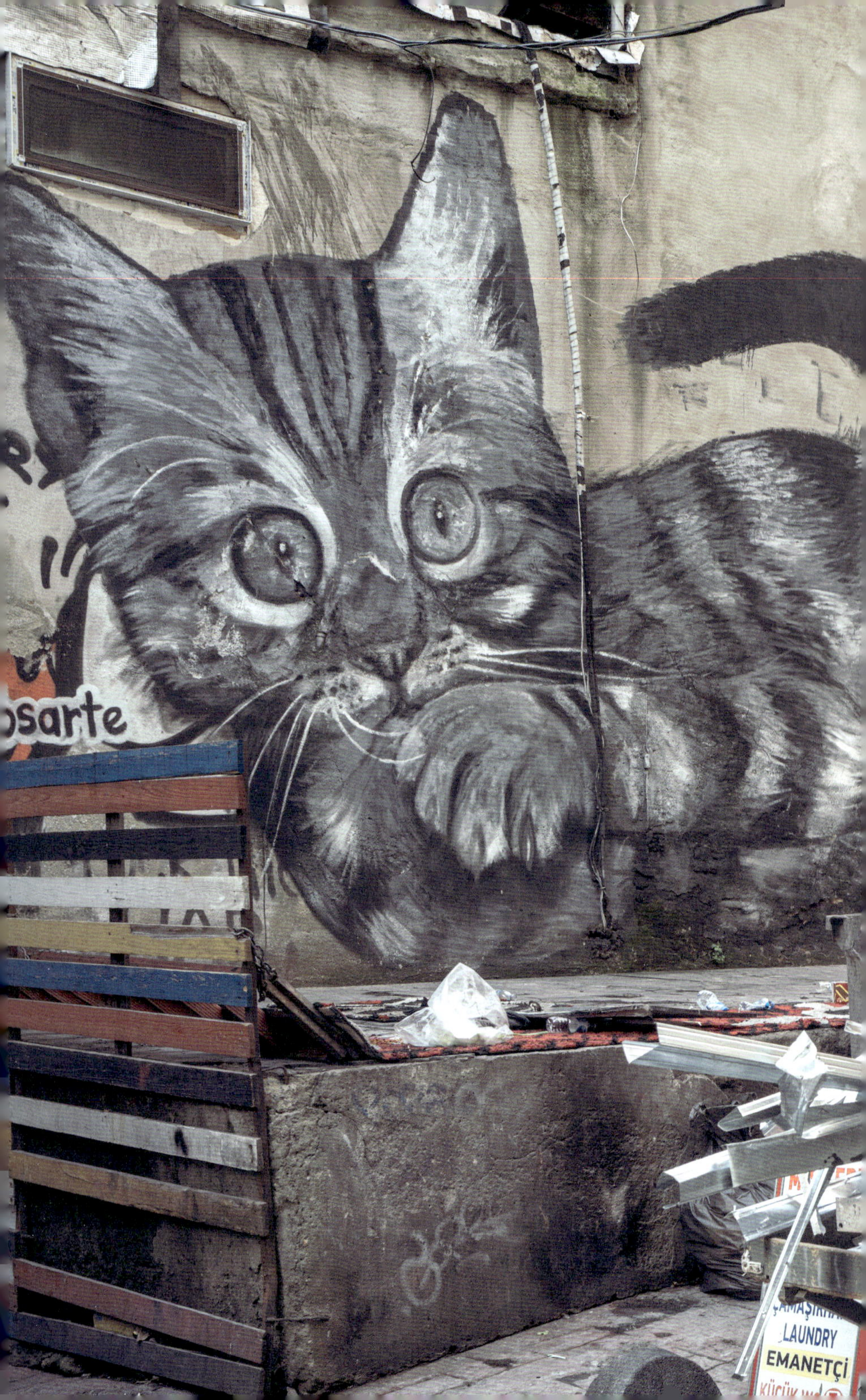
osarte
LAUNDRY
EMANETÇİ

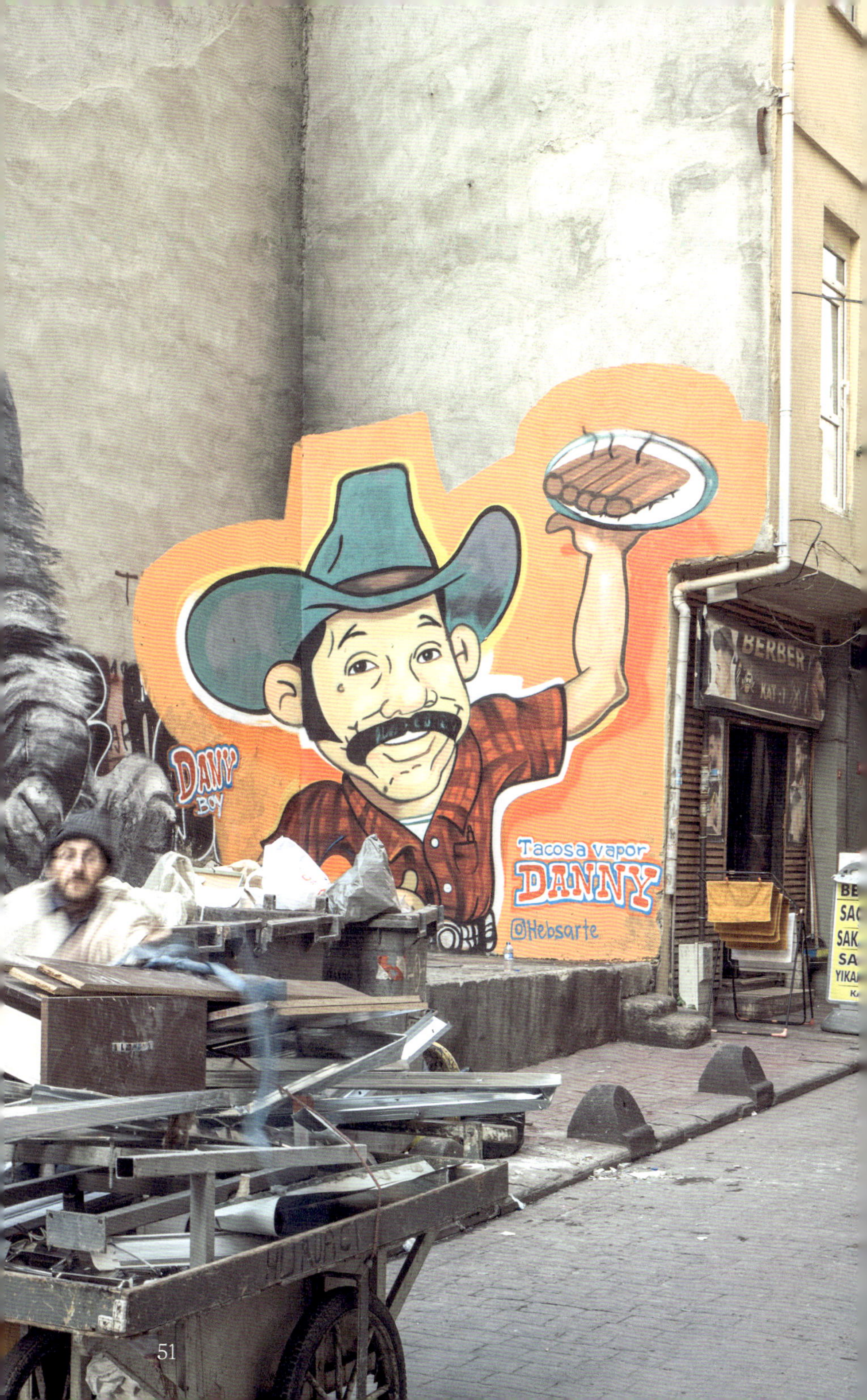
DANY
BOY
Tacosa vapor
DANNY
@Hebsarte
BERBER

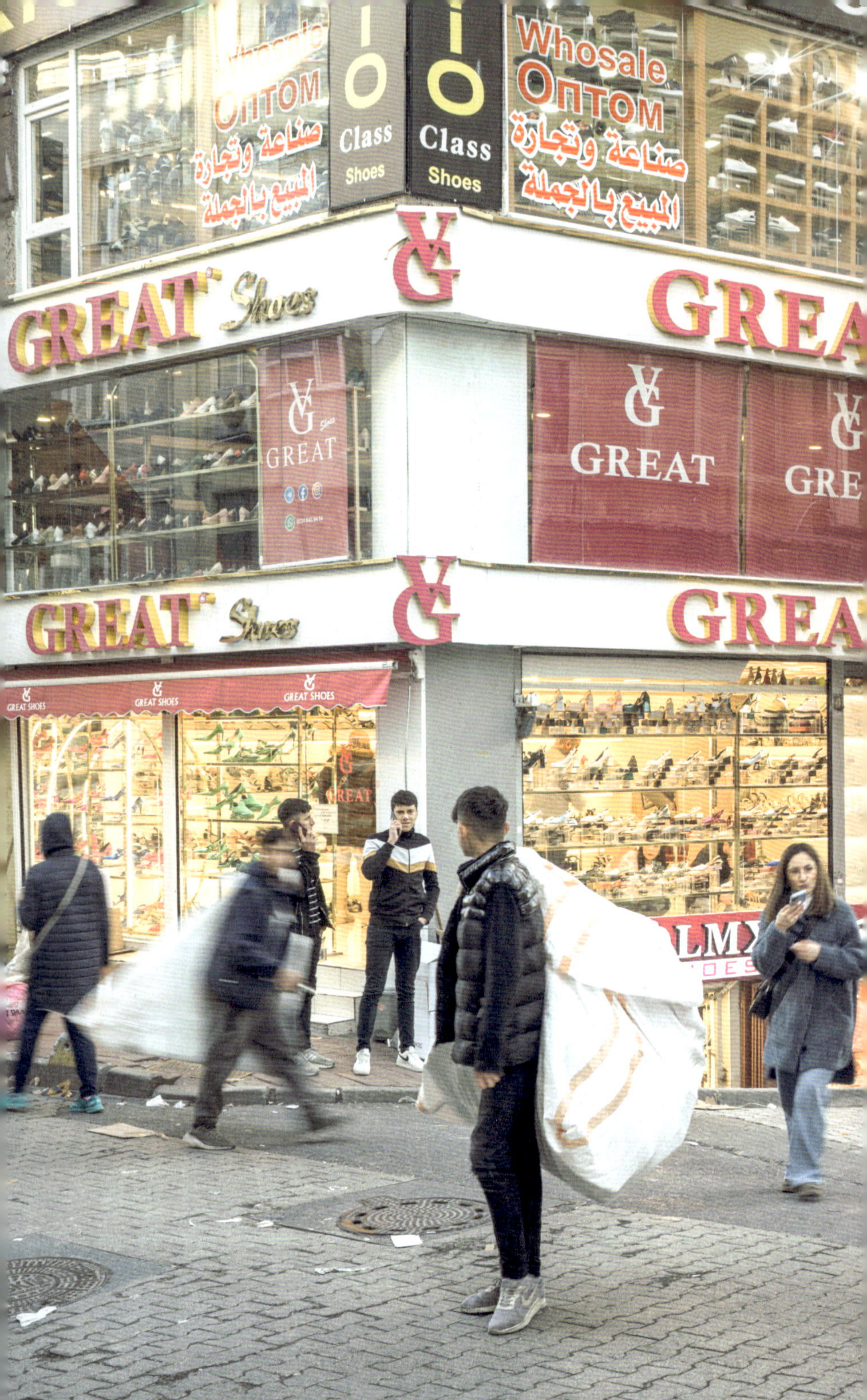
Whosale
ОПТОМ
صناعة وتجارة
المبيع بالجملة
Class
Shoes
GREAT Shoes
GREAT
GREAT SHOES
LMX

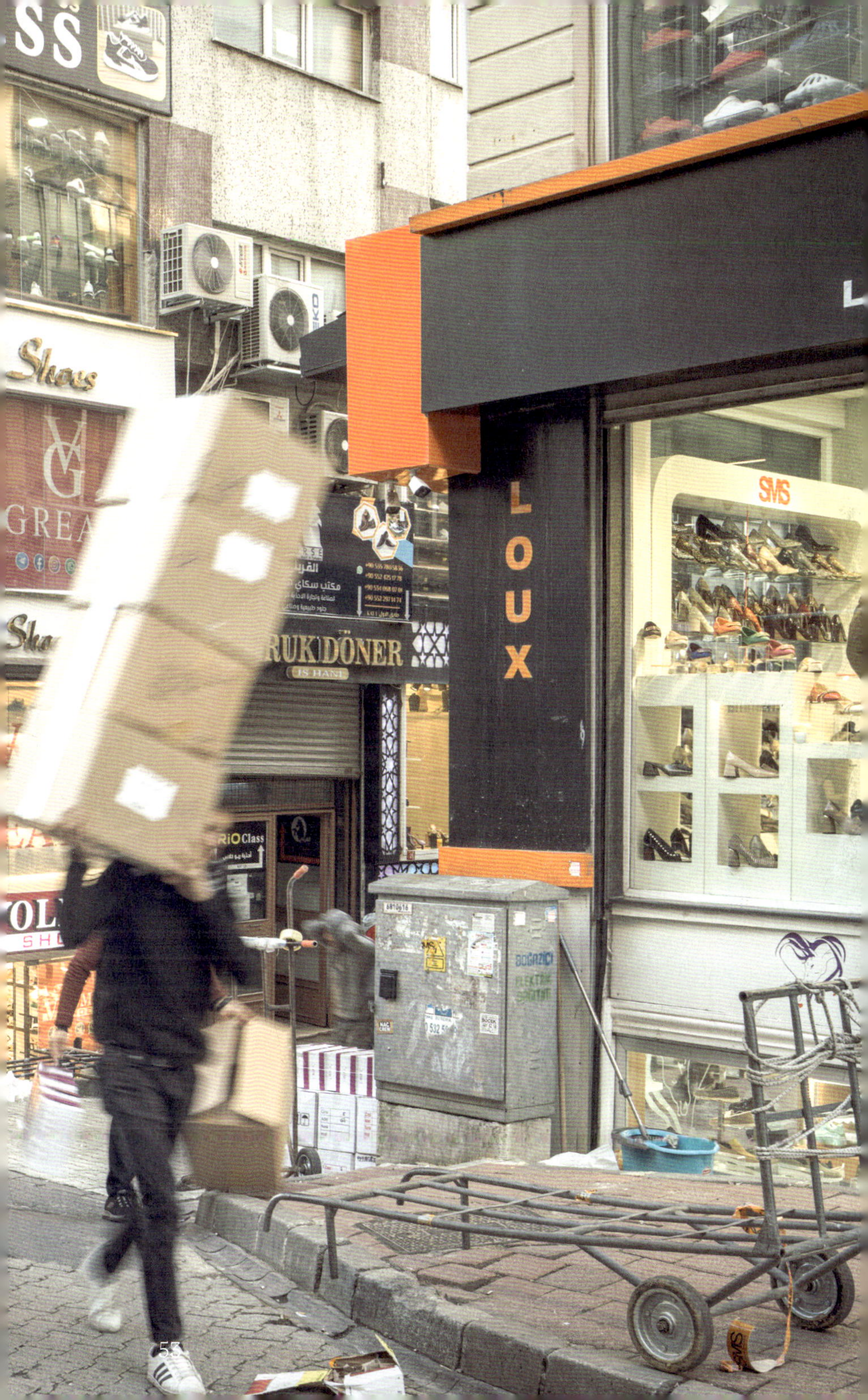
LOUX
SMS
Shoes
RUK DÖNER
RiO Class

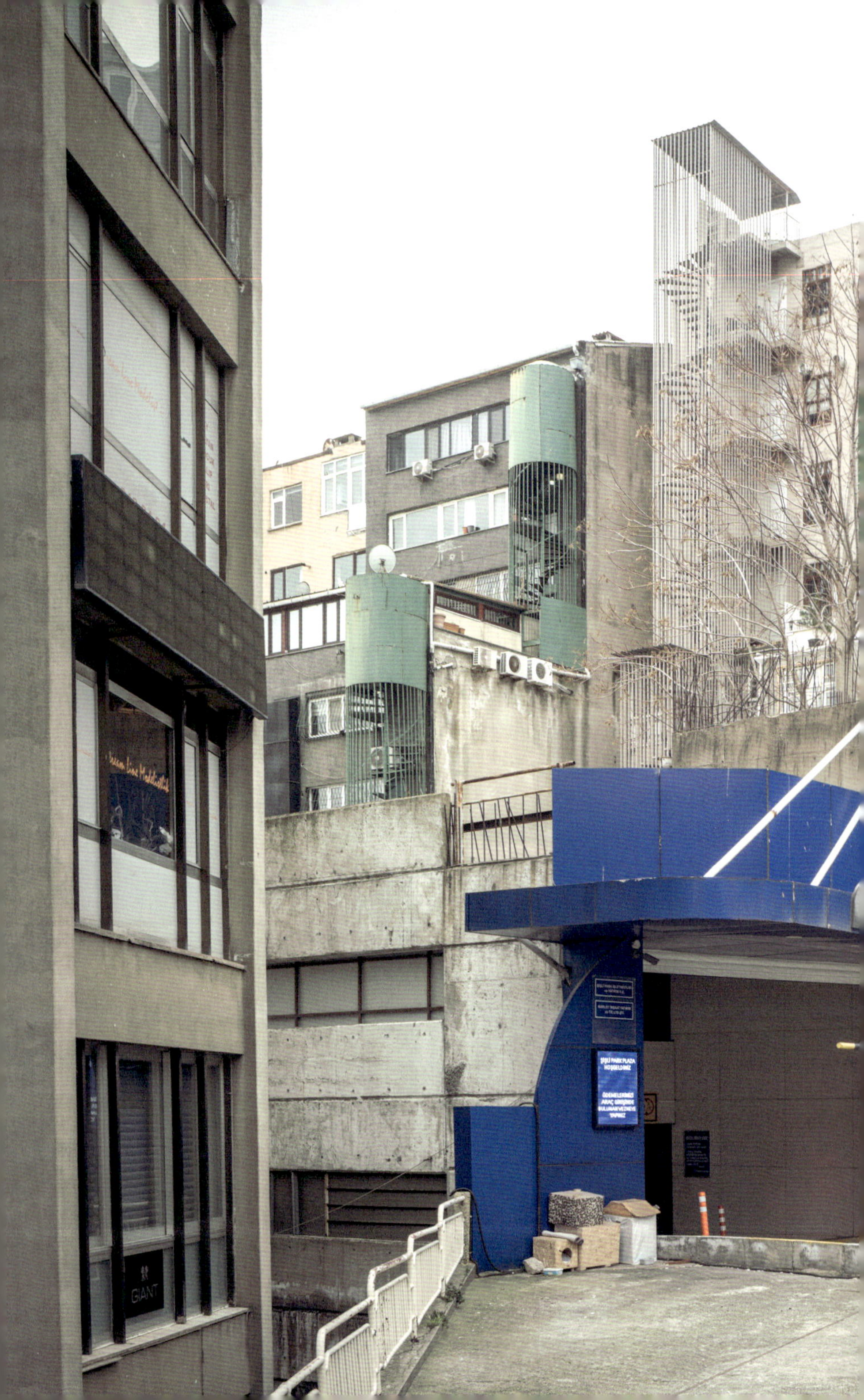
ŞİŞLİ PARK PLAZA
HOŞGELDİNİZ
ÖDEMELERİNİZİ
ARAÇ GİRİŞİNDE
BULUNAN VEZNEYE
YAPINIZ
GIANT

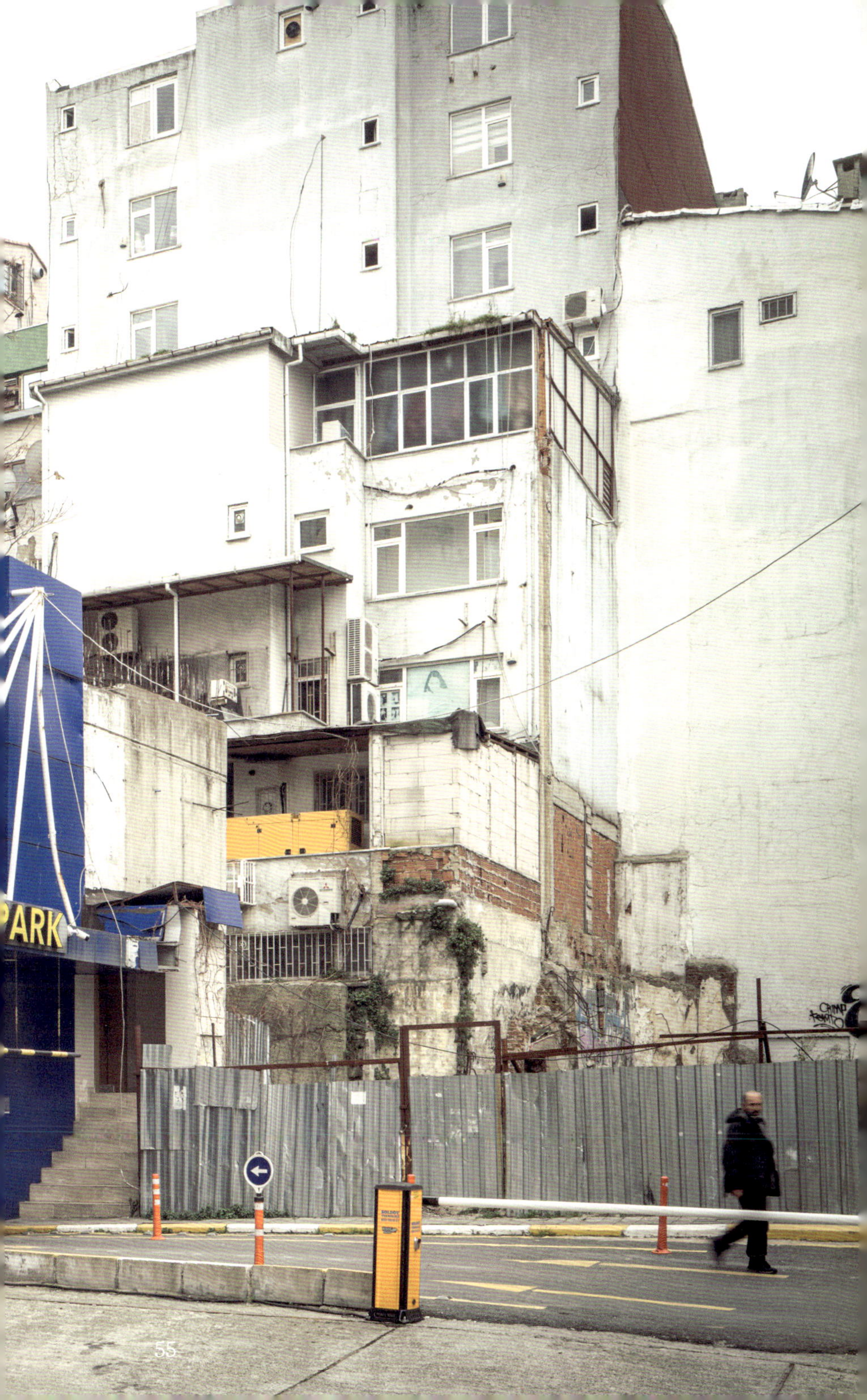
PARK

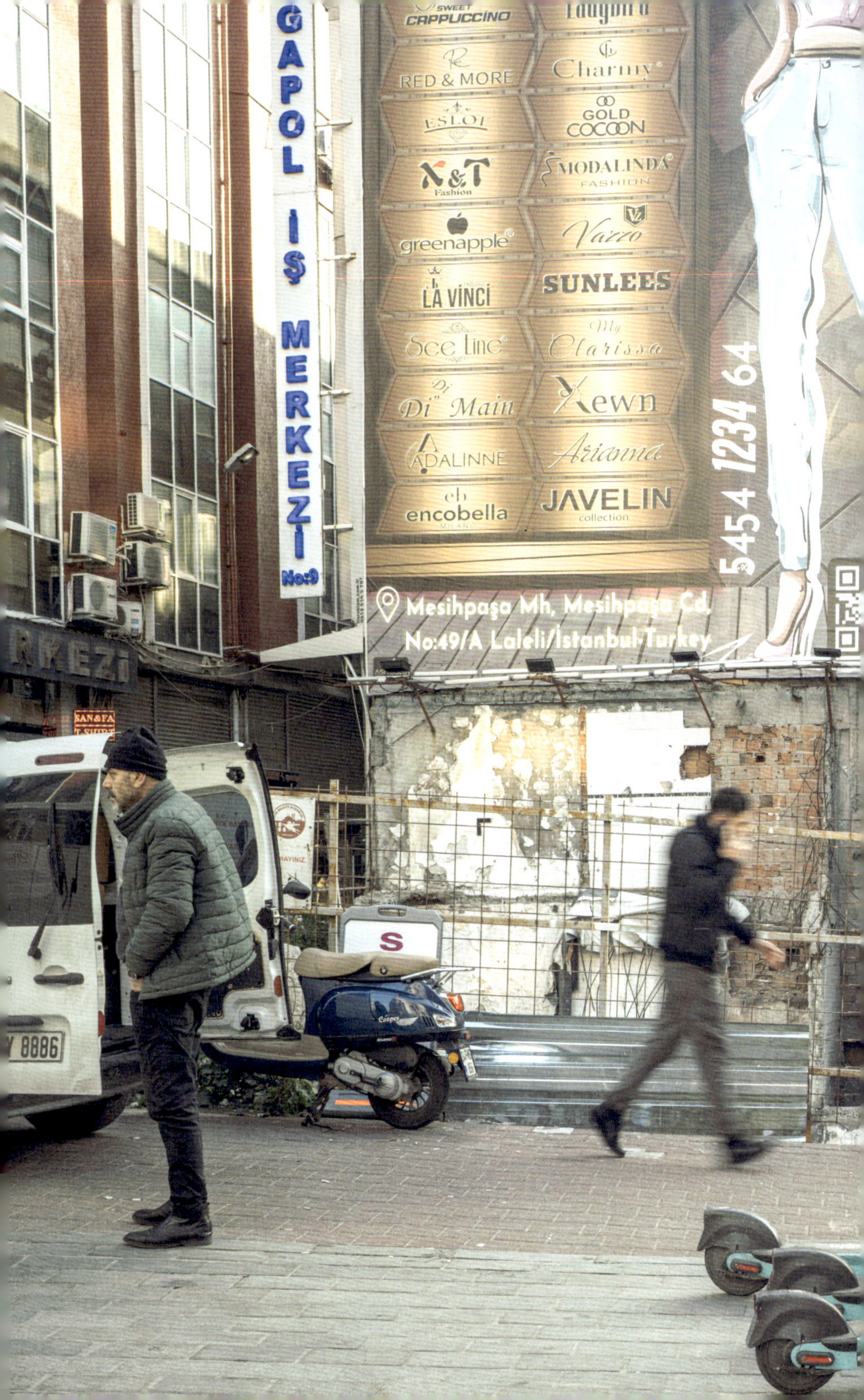
GAPOL İŞ MERKEZİ
No:9
SWEET CAPPUCCINO
RED & MORE
Charmy
GOLD COCOON
X&T Fashion
MODALINDA FASHION
greenapple
Vazzo
LA VINCI
SUNLEES
See line
My Clarissa
Di Di" Main
Xewn
ADALINNE
Arianna
encobella
JAVELIN collection
5454 1234 64
Mesihpaşa Mh, Mesihpaşa Cd,
No:49/A Laleli/İstanbul-Turkey
RKEZİ
Y 8886
S

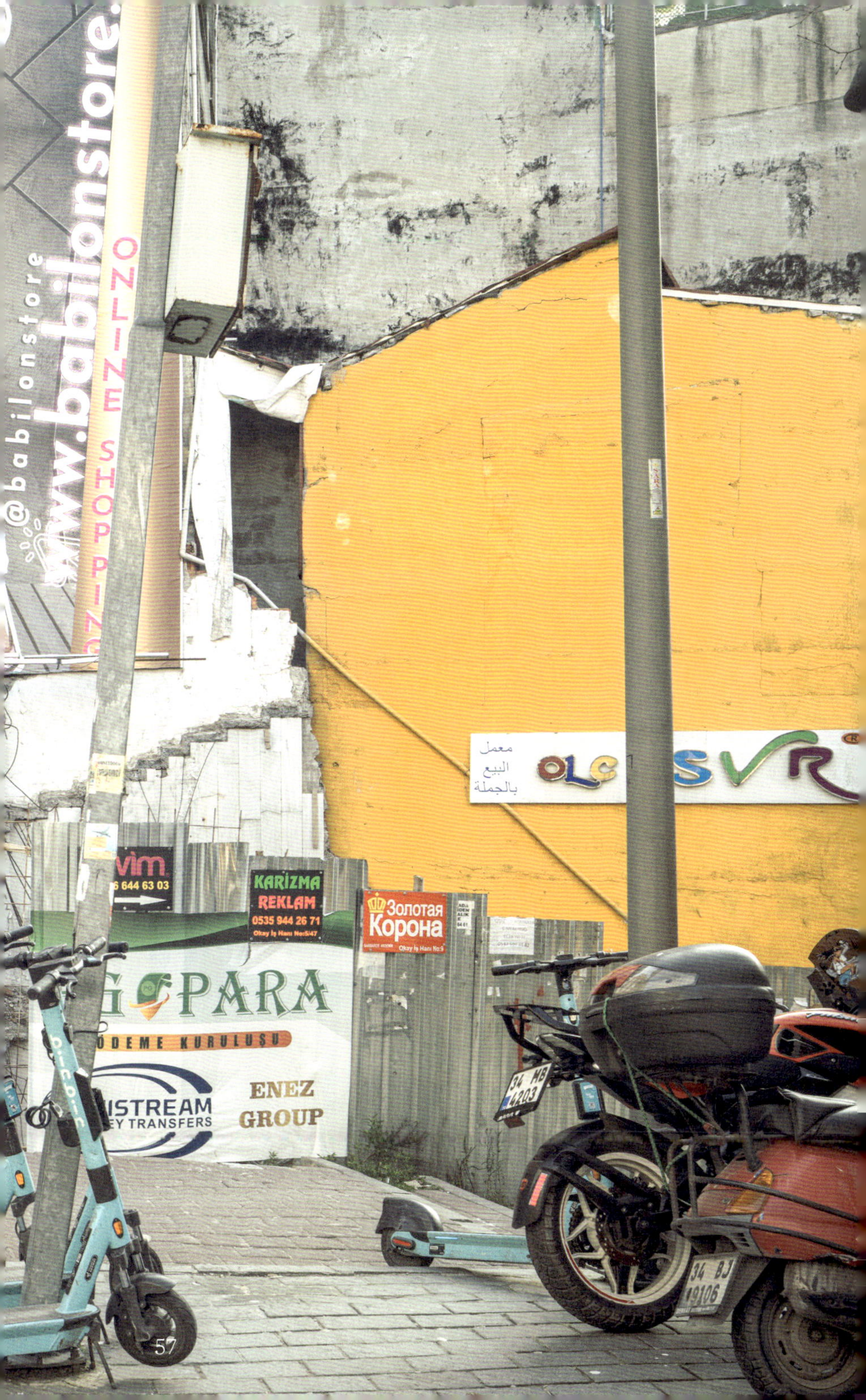
www.babilonstore.
@babilonstore
KARIZMA
REKLAM
0535 944 26 71
Золотая
Корона
معمل
البيع
بالجملة
PARA
ENEZ
GROUP

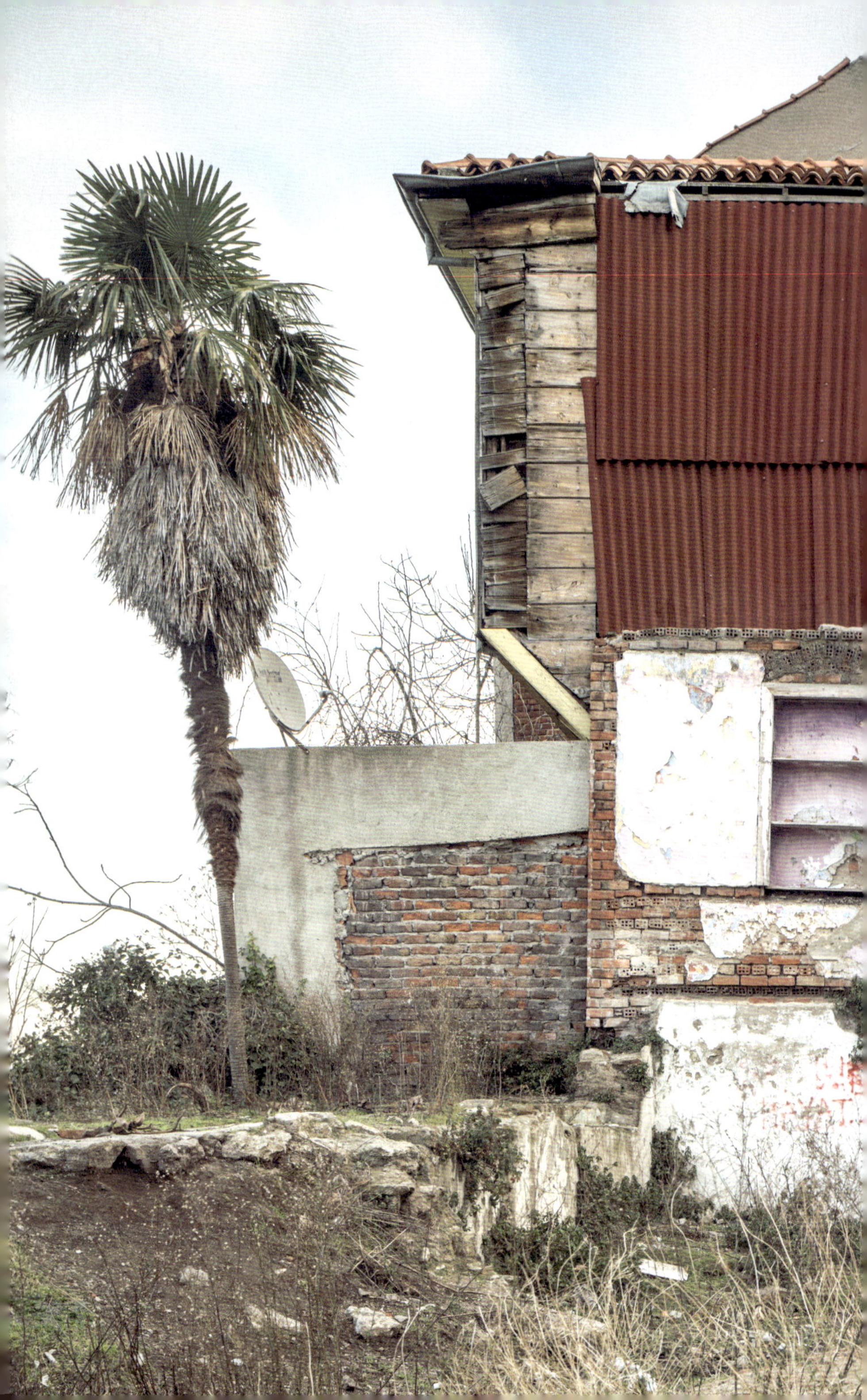

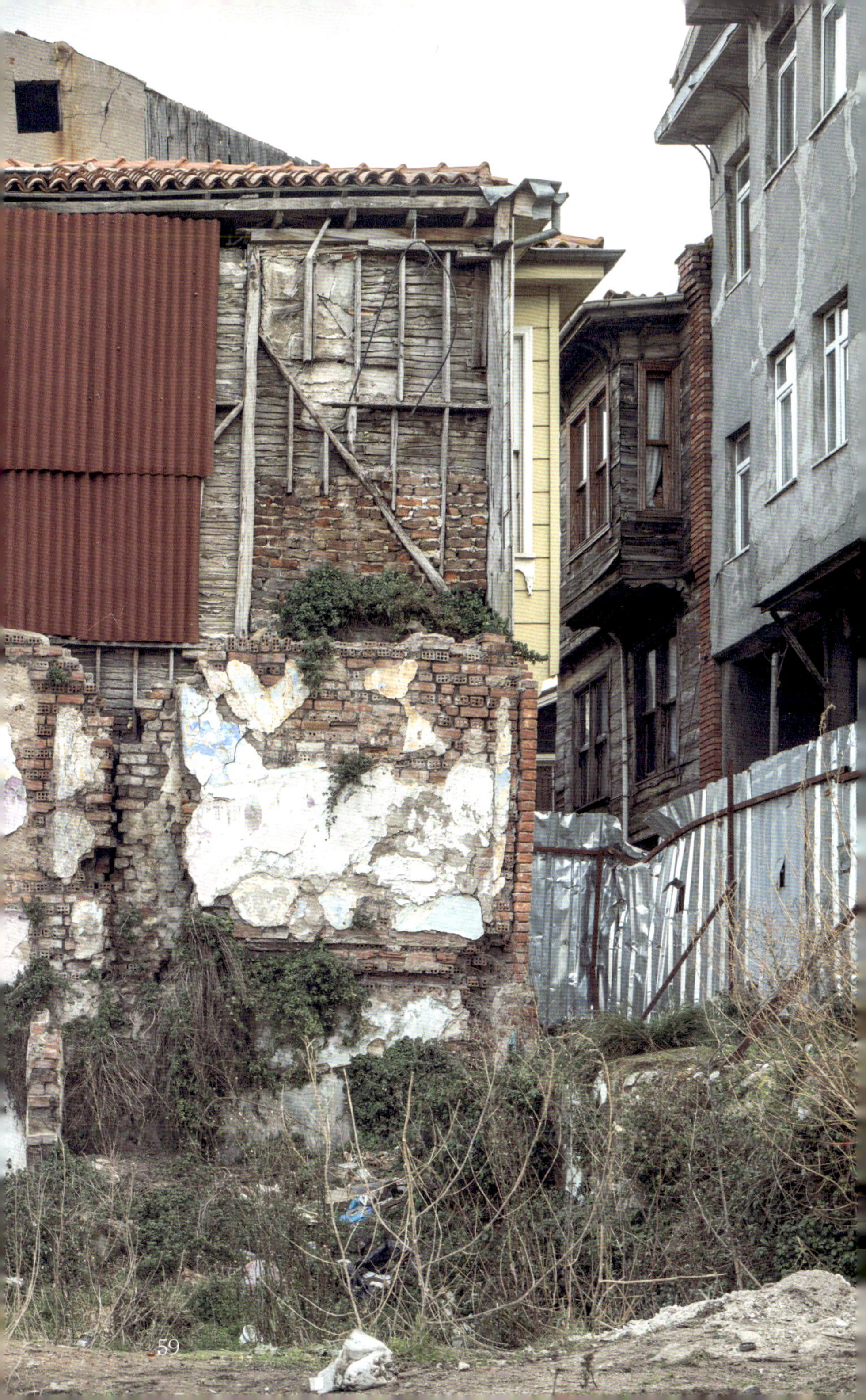

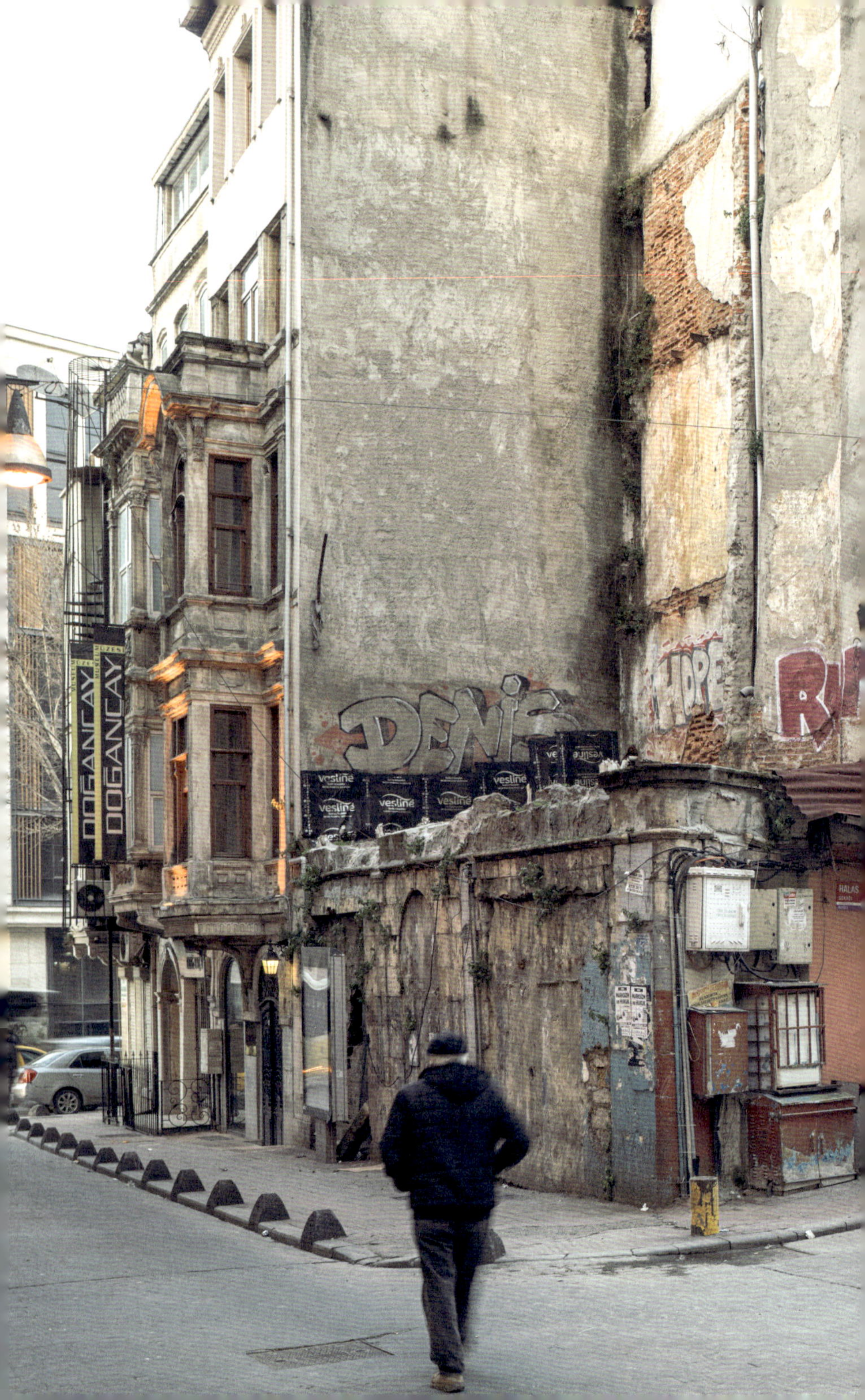

DOĞANÇAY
DOĞANÇAY
vesline
HALAS

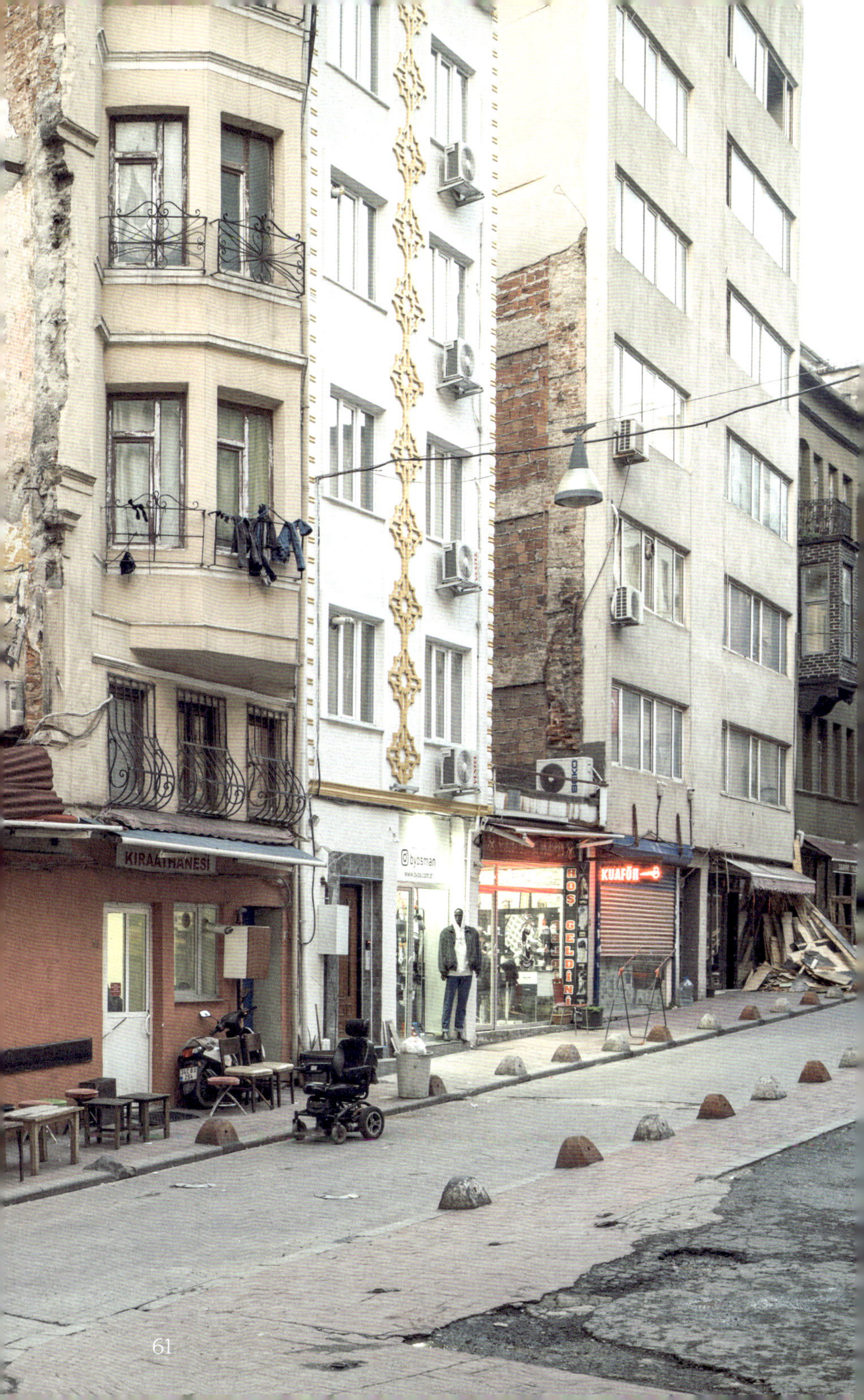
KIRAATHANESI
byosman
www.byos.com.tr
HOŞ GELDİNİ
KUAFÖR
BEKO

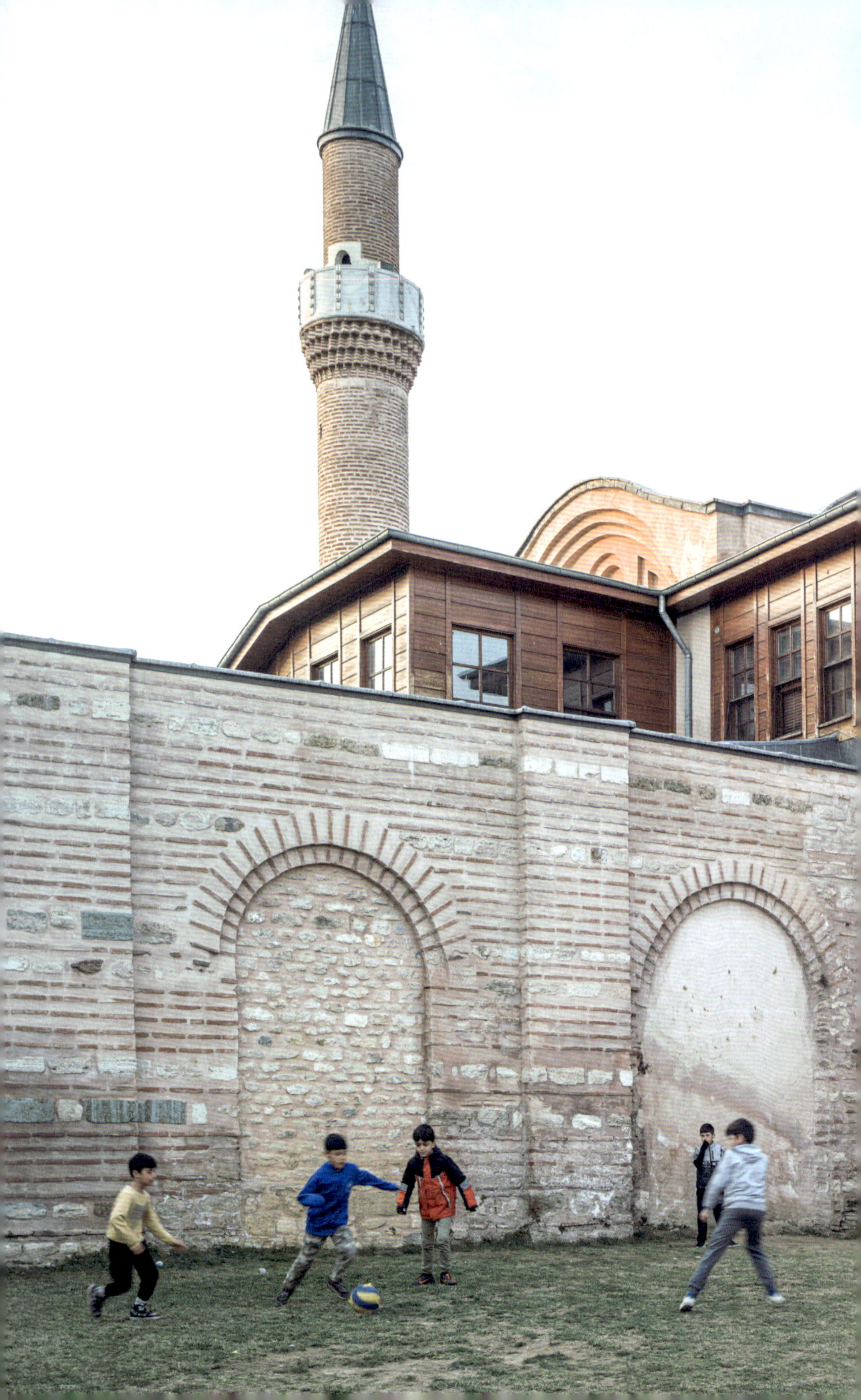

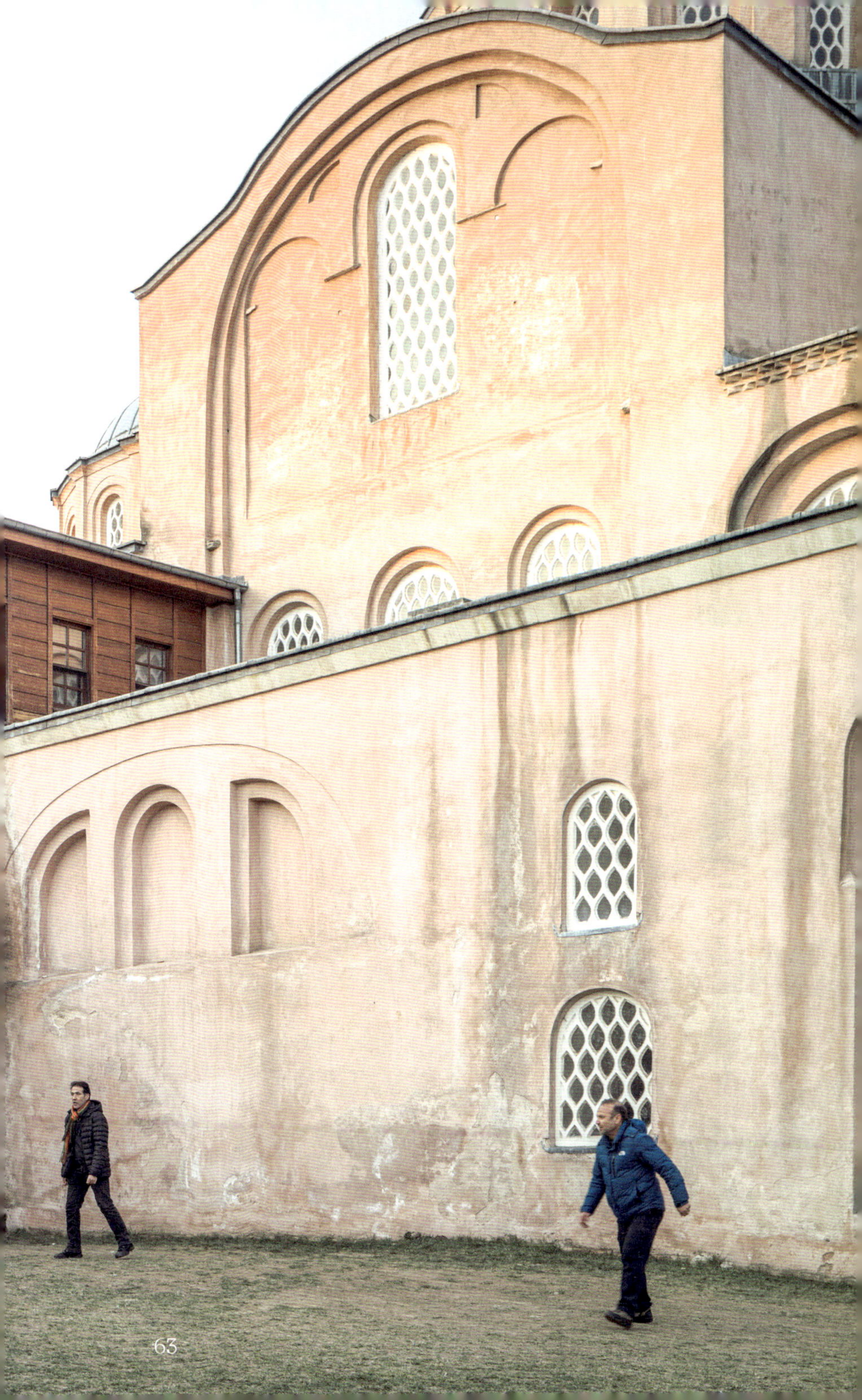

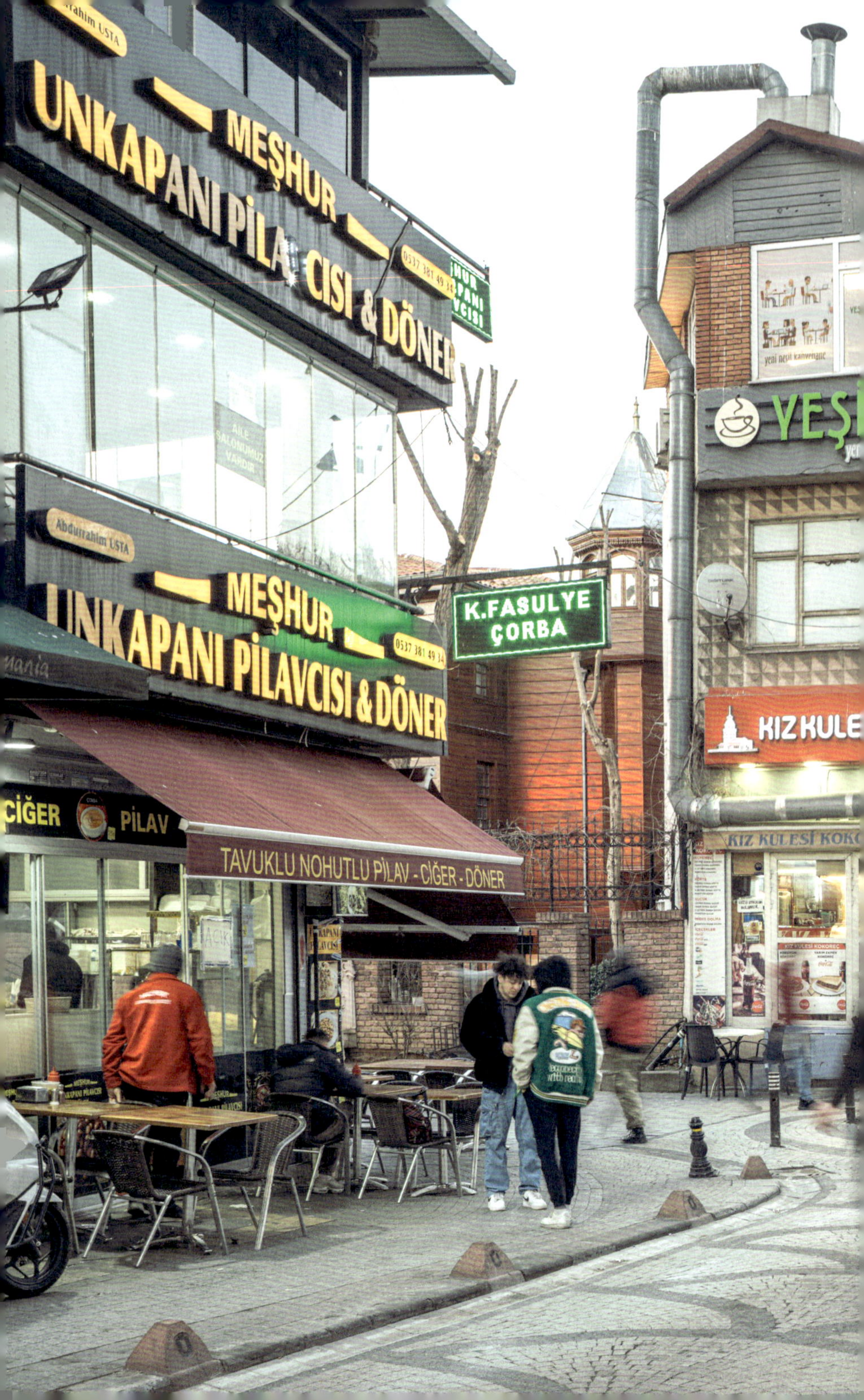
MEŞHUR
UNKAPANI PİLA CISI & DÖNER
0537 381 49 34
Abdurrahim USTA
MEŞHUR
UNKAPANI PİLAVCISI & DÖNER
0537 381 49 34
K.FASULYE
ÇORBA
CİĞER
PİLAV
TAVUKLU NOHUTLU PİLAV - CİĞER - DÖNER
KIZ KULE
YEŞİ

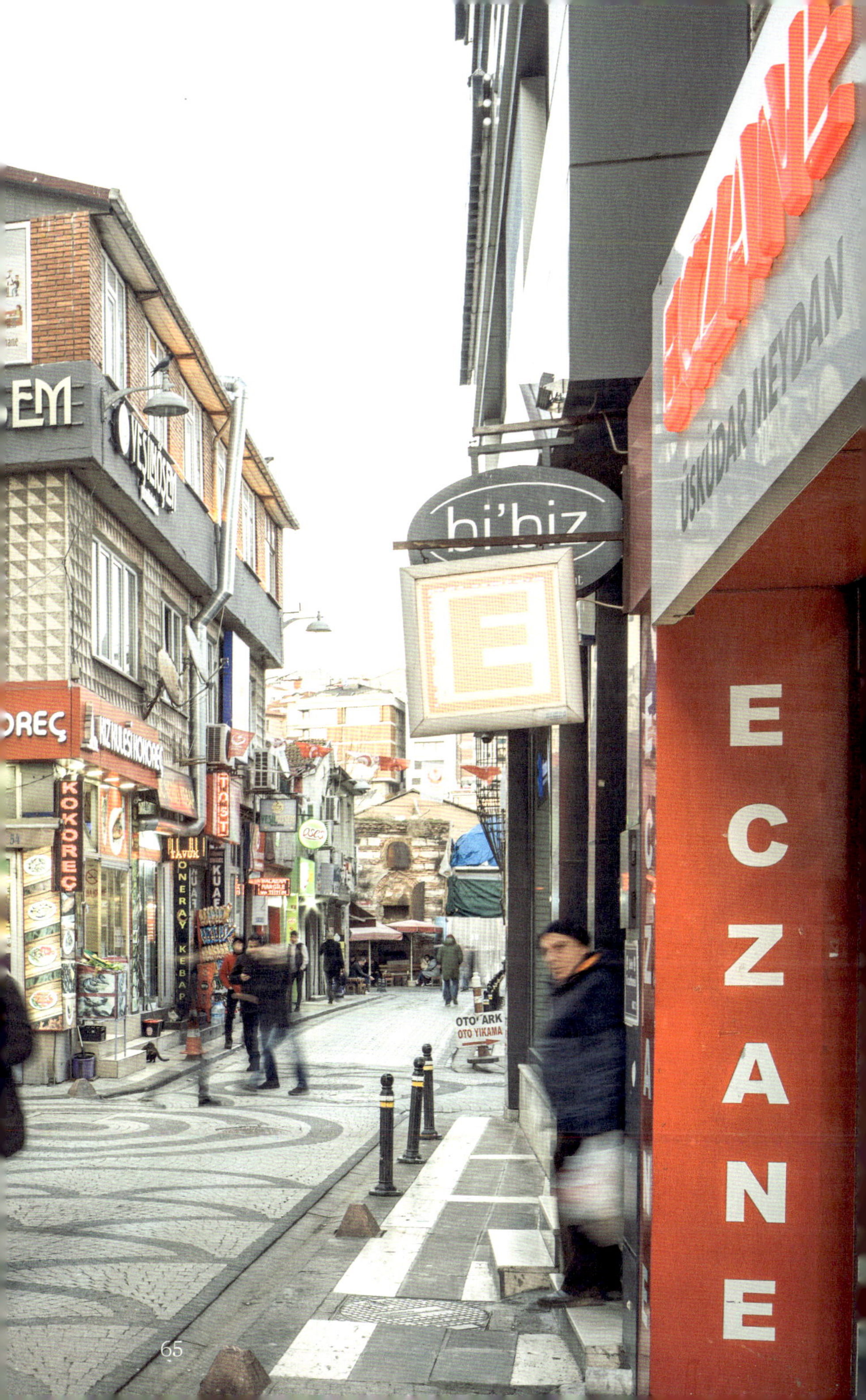
ÜSKÜDAR MEYDAN
bi'biz
E
ECZANE
EM
OREÇ
KOKOREÇ
KEBAP
OTO YIKAMA

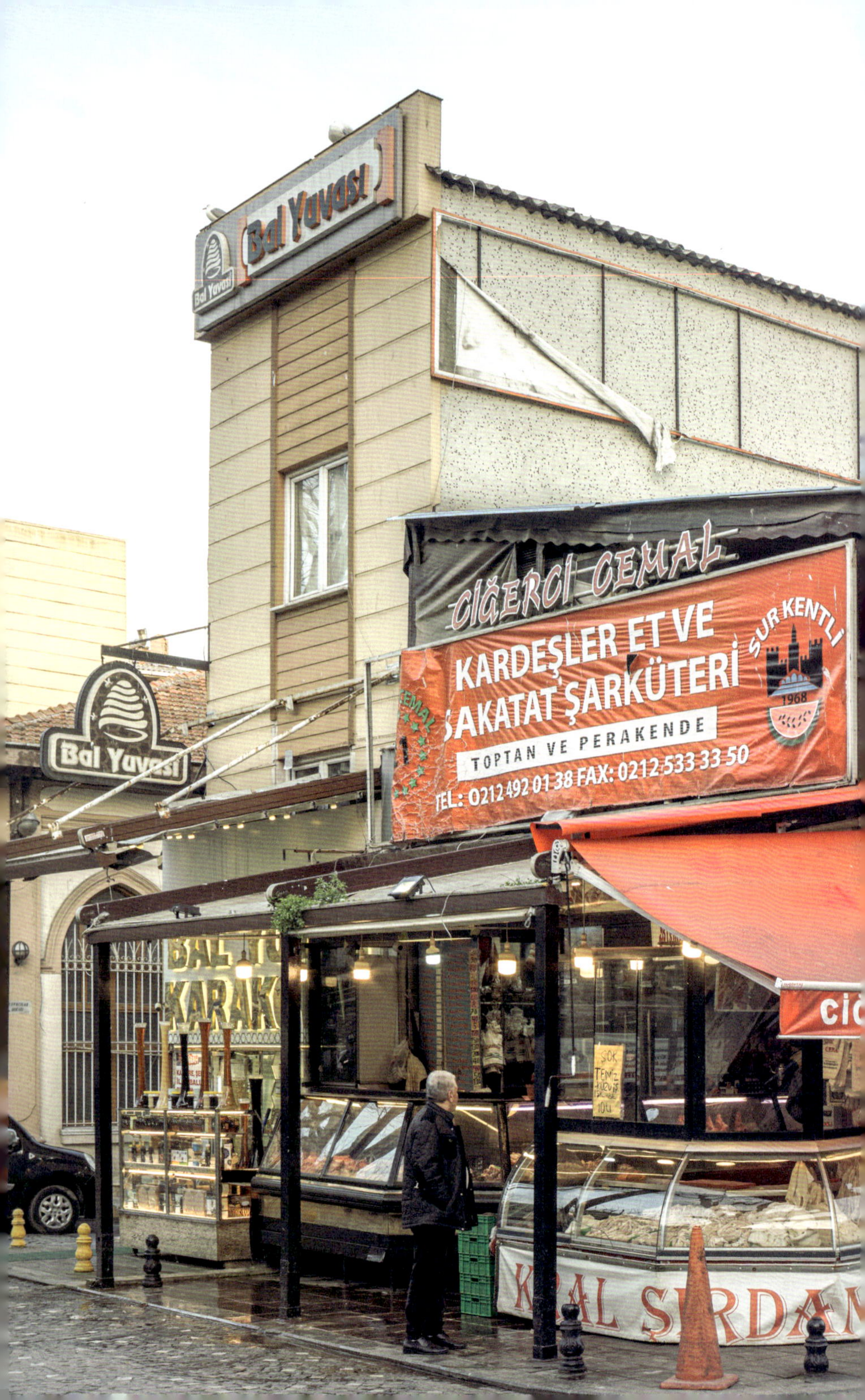
Bal Yavası
Bal Yavası
Bal Yavası
CİĞERCİ CEMAL
KARDEŞLER ET VE
SAKATAT ŞARKÜTERİ
TOPTAN VE PERAKENDE
TEL: 0212 492 01 38 FAX: 0212 533 33 50
SUR KENTLİ
1968
KRAL SERDAN

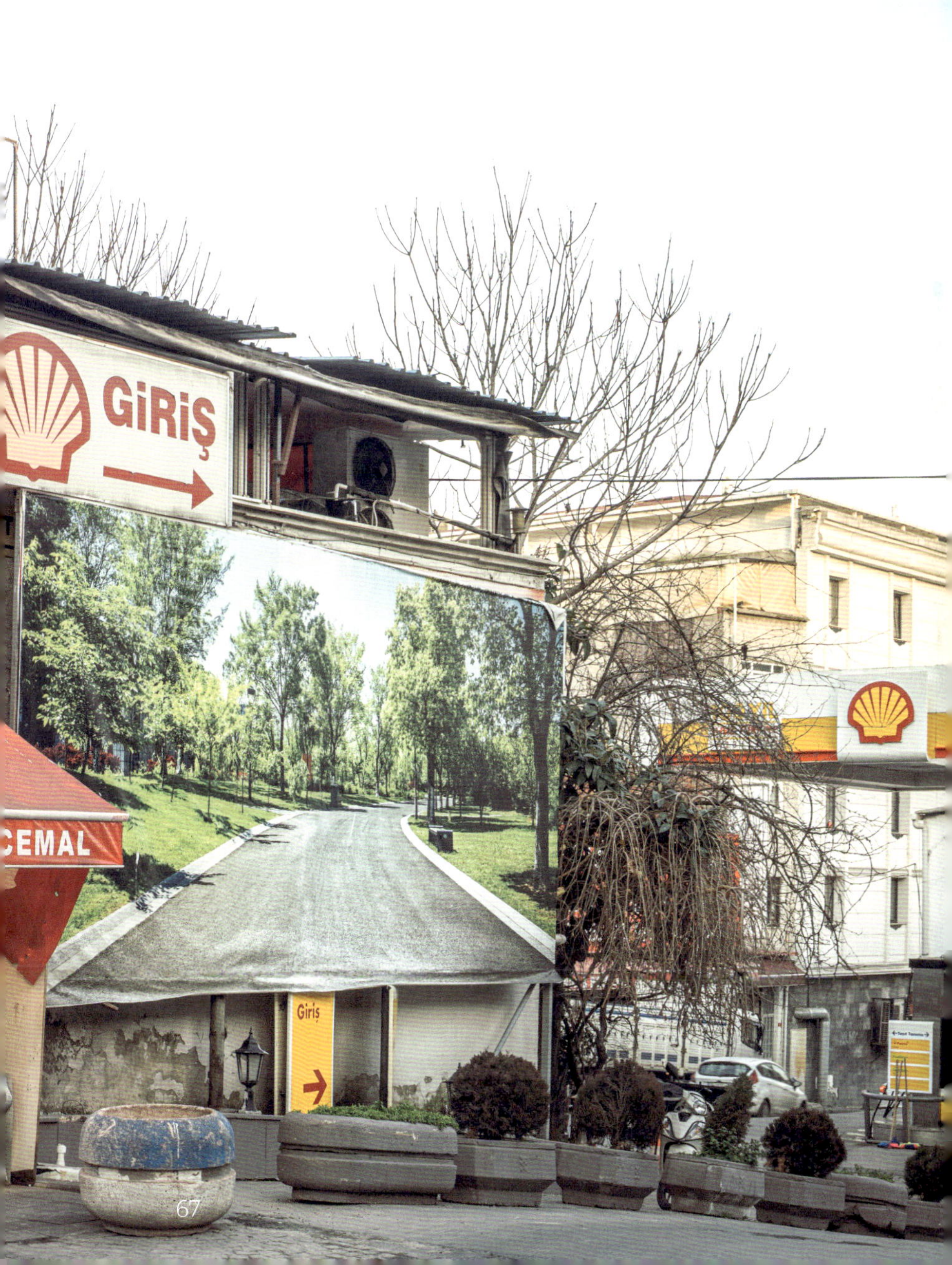
GiRiŞ
CEMAL
Giriş

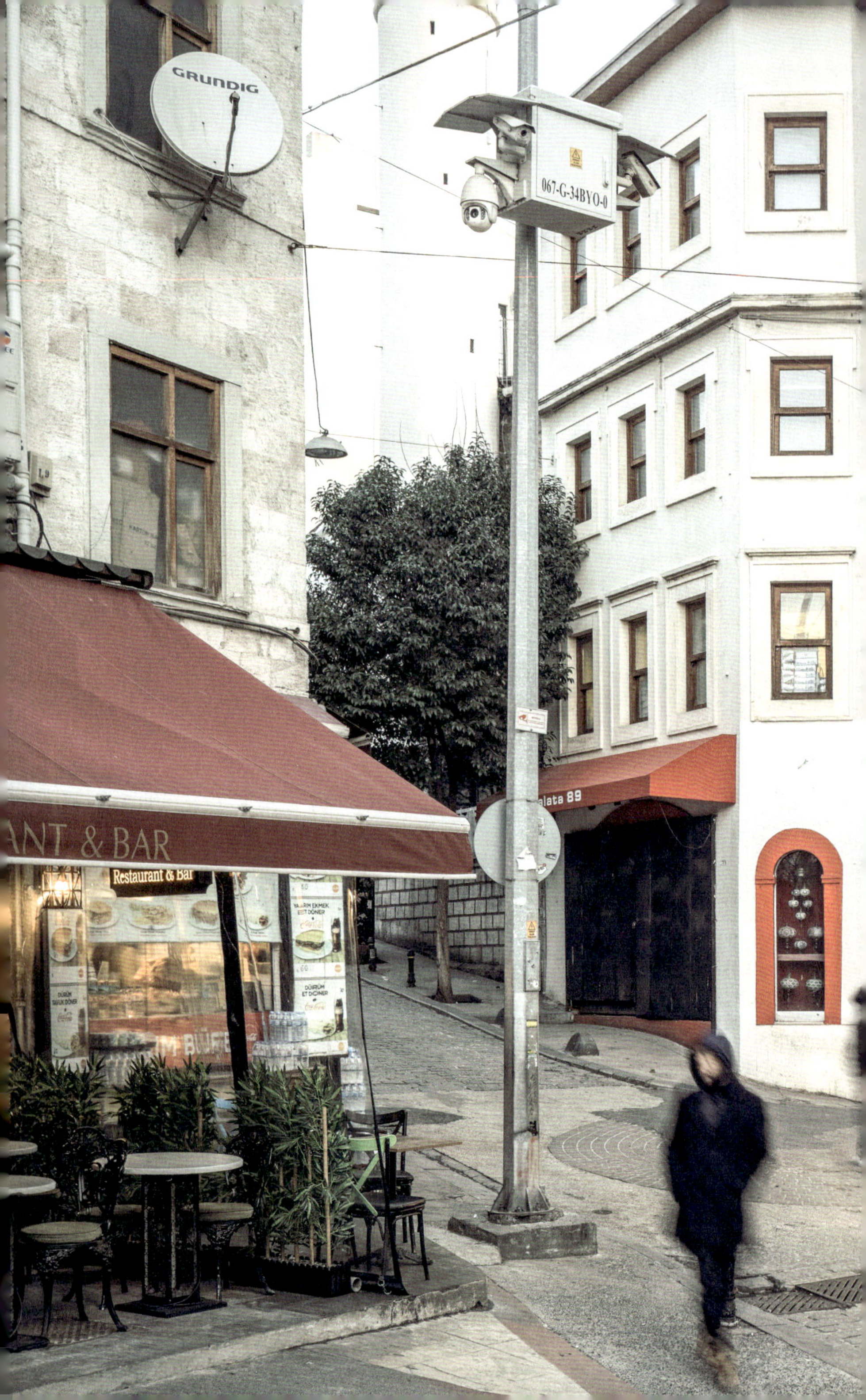
GRUNDIG
067-G-34BYO-0
ANT & BAR
Restaurant & Bar
YARIM EKMEK
ET DÖNER
DÜRÜM
ET DÖNER
DÜRÜM
TAVUK DÖNER
alata 89

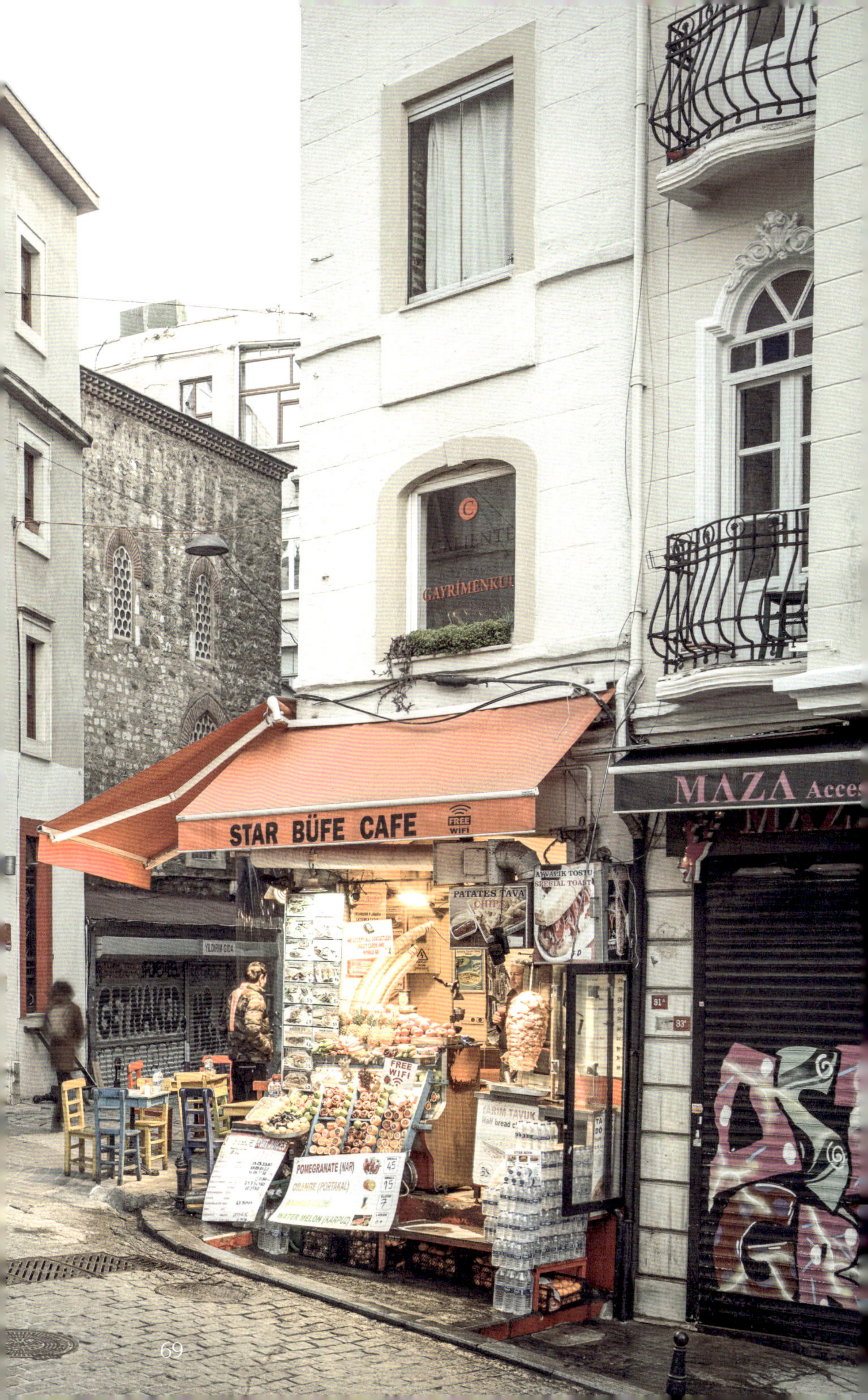

STAR BÜFE CAFE
FREE WIFI
MAZA
PATATES TAVA
CHIPS
FREE WIFI
POMEGRANATE (NAR)
ORANGE (PORTAKAL)
WATER MELON (KARPUZ)
YILDIRIM GIDA

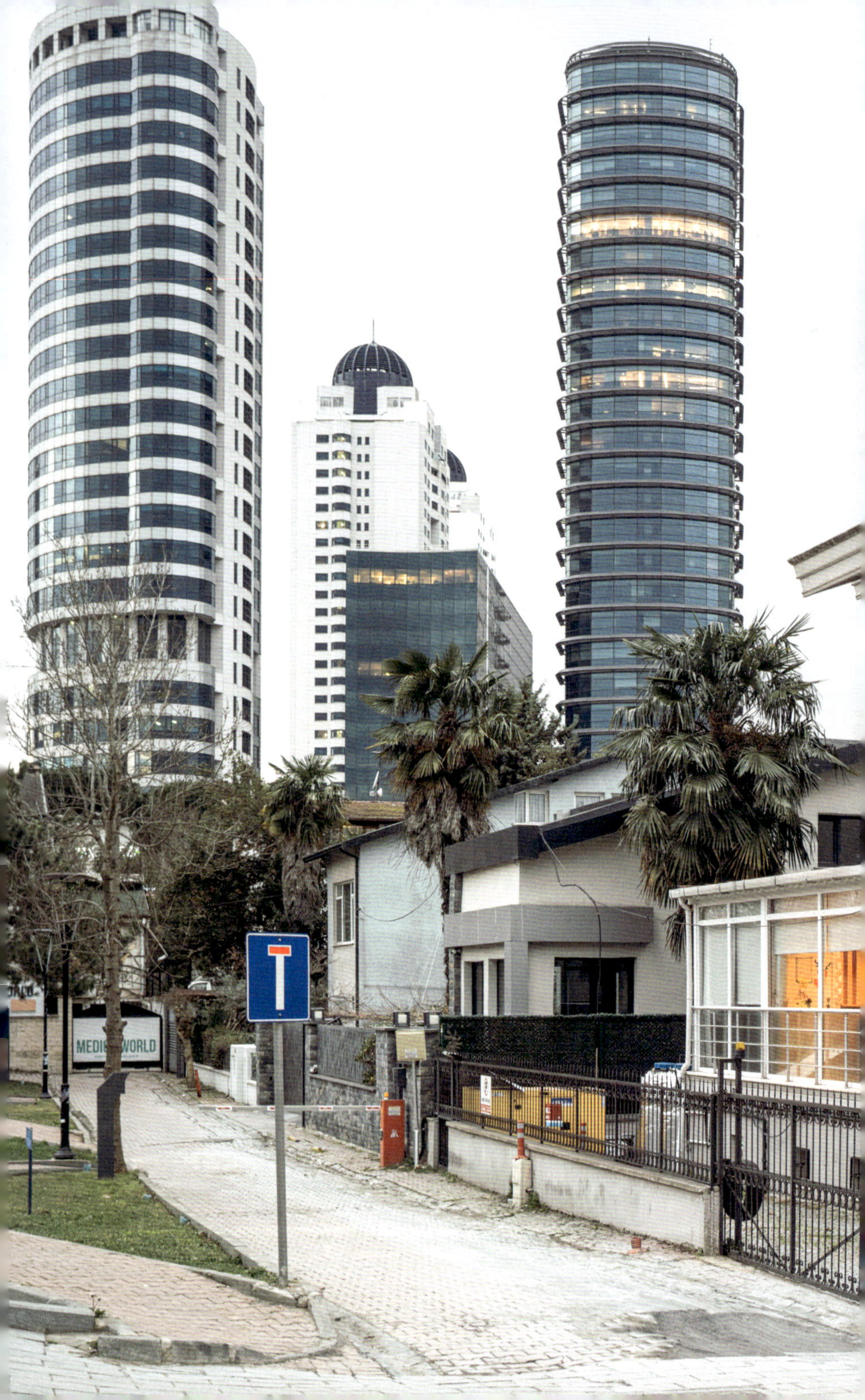

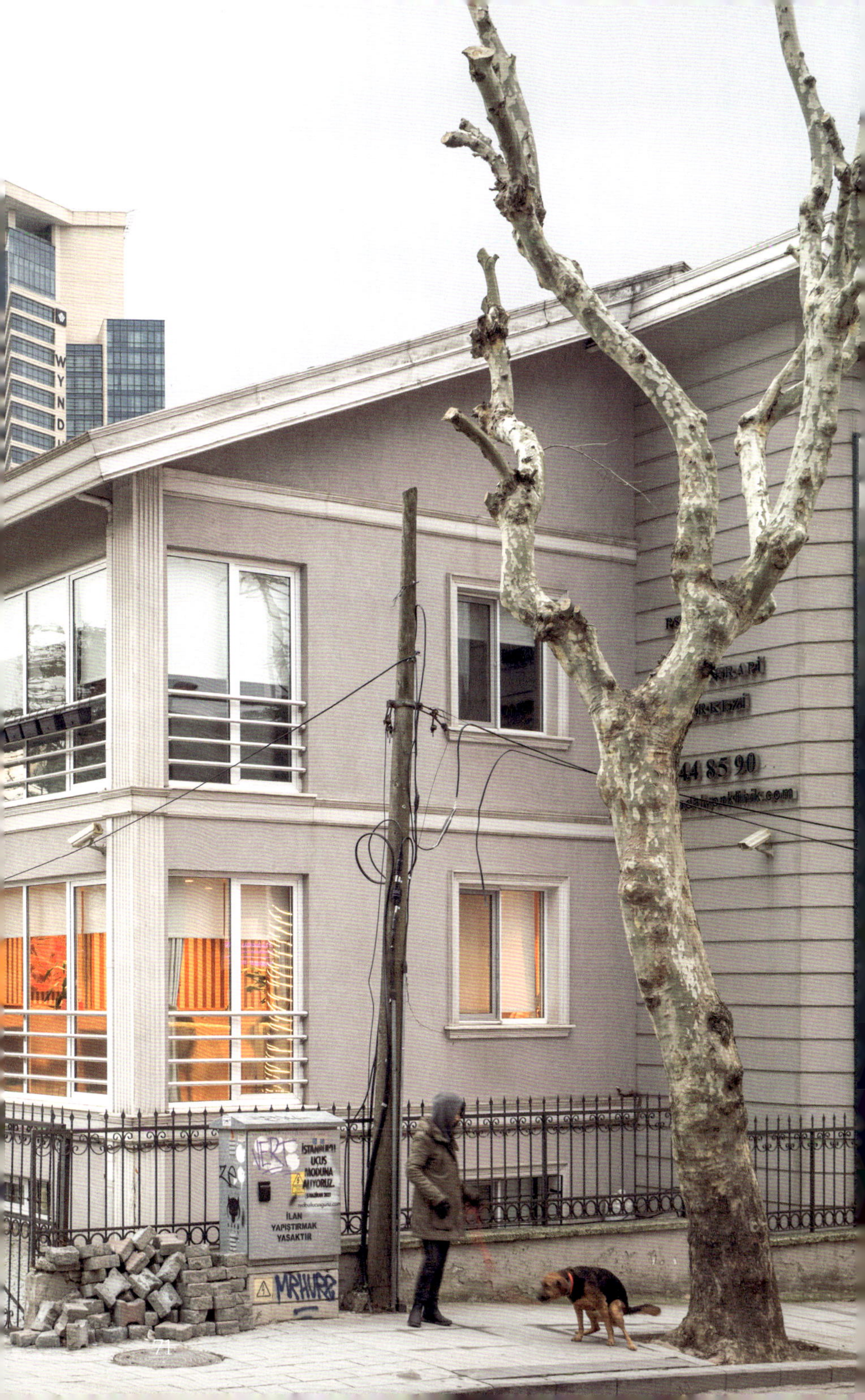
İLAN
YAPIŞTIRMAK
YASAKTIR
44 85 90

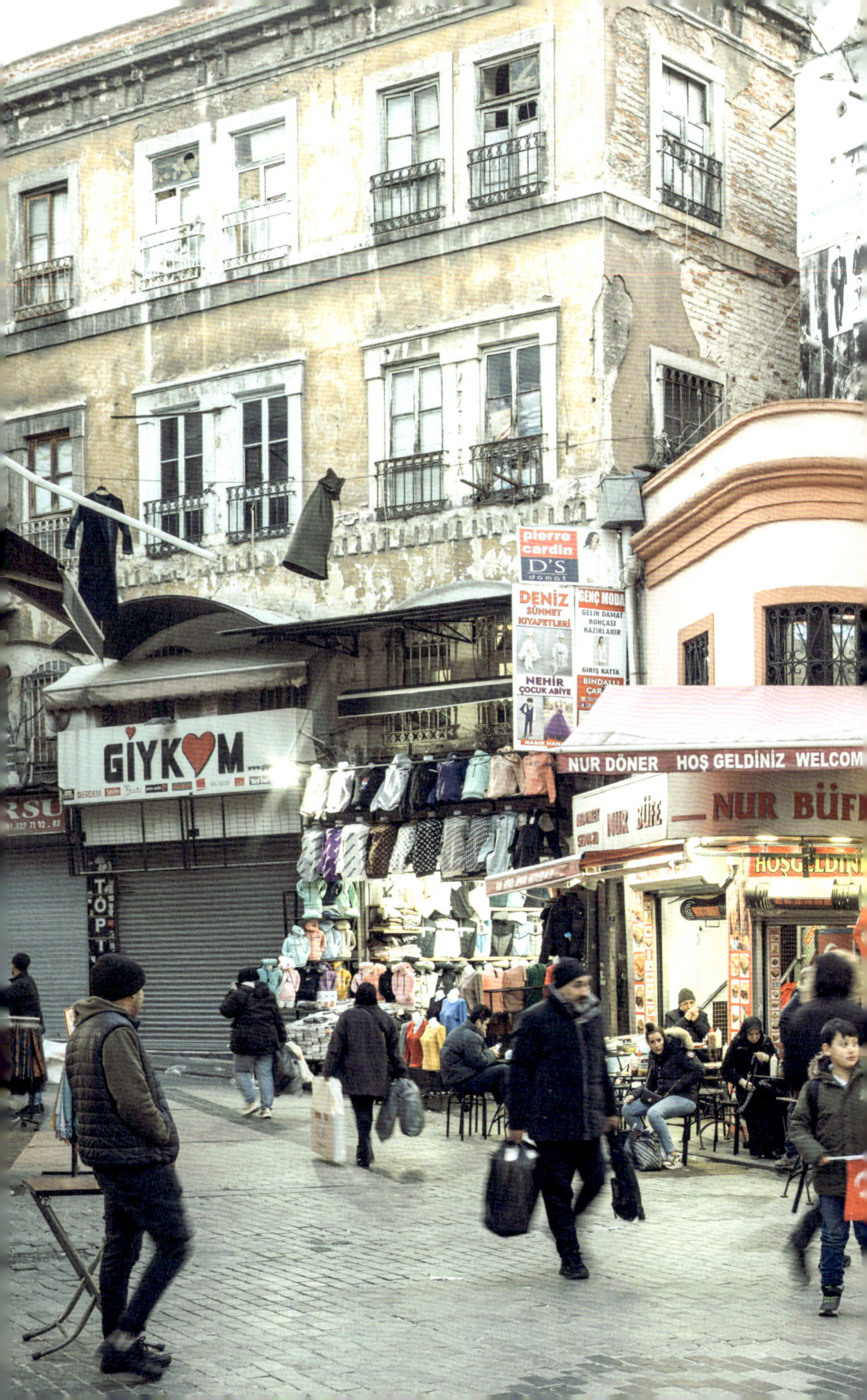

pierre cardin
D'S damat
DENIZ
SÜNNET
KIYAFETLERİ
GENÇ MODA
GELİN DAMAT
BOHÇASI
HAZIRLANIR
GİRİŞ KATTA
NEHİR
ÇOCUK ABİYE
GİYK♥M
NUR DÖNER
HOŞ GELDİNİZ
NUR BÜFE

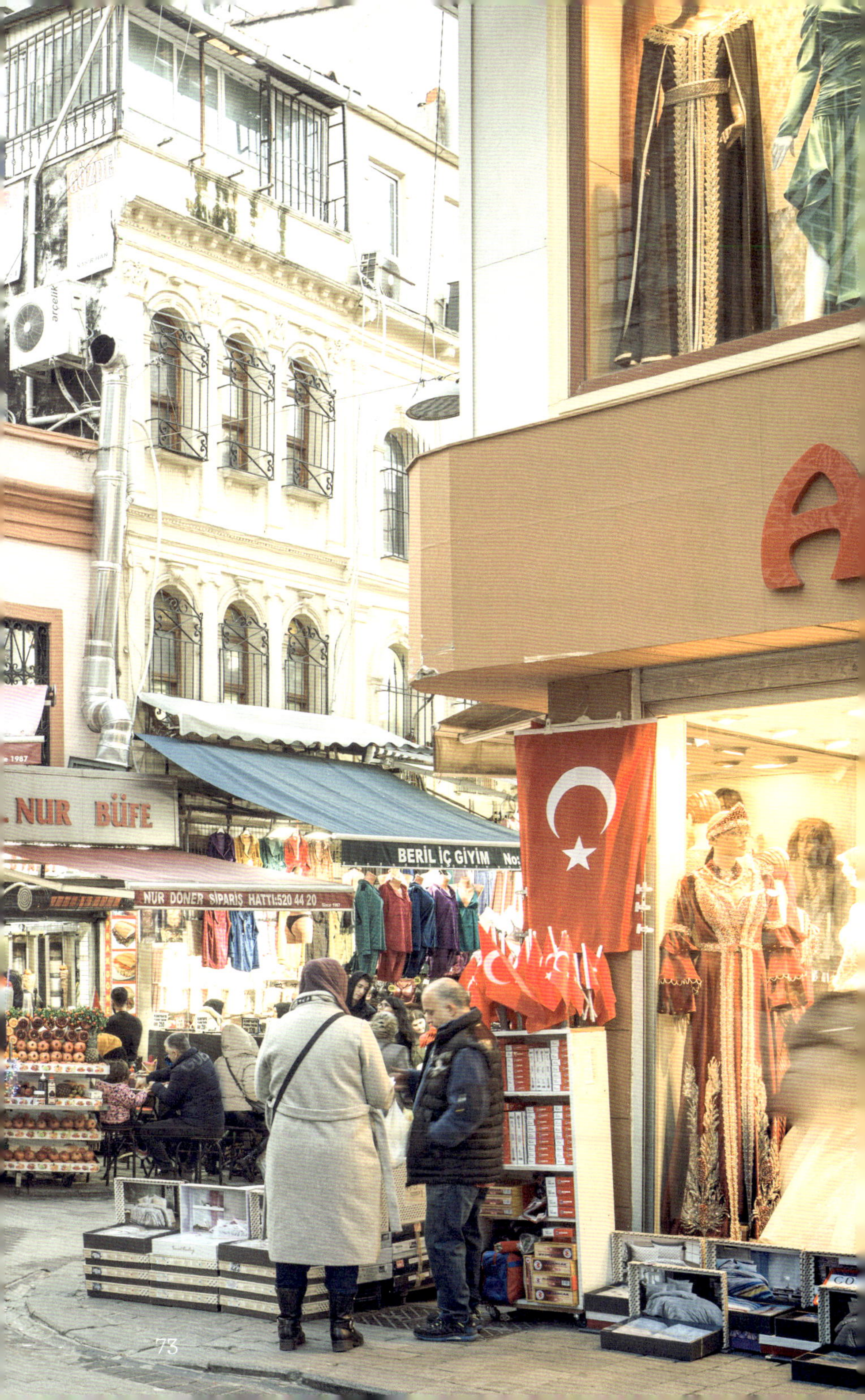
NUR BÜFE
BERIL İÇ GIYIM No:
NUR DÖNER SIPARIŞ HATTI:520 44 20

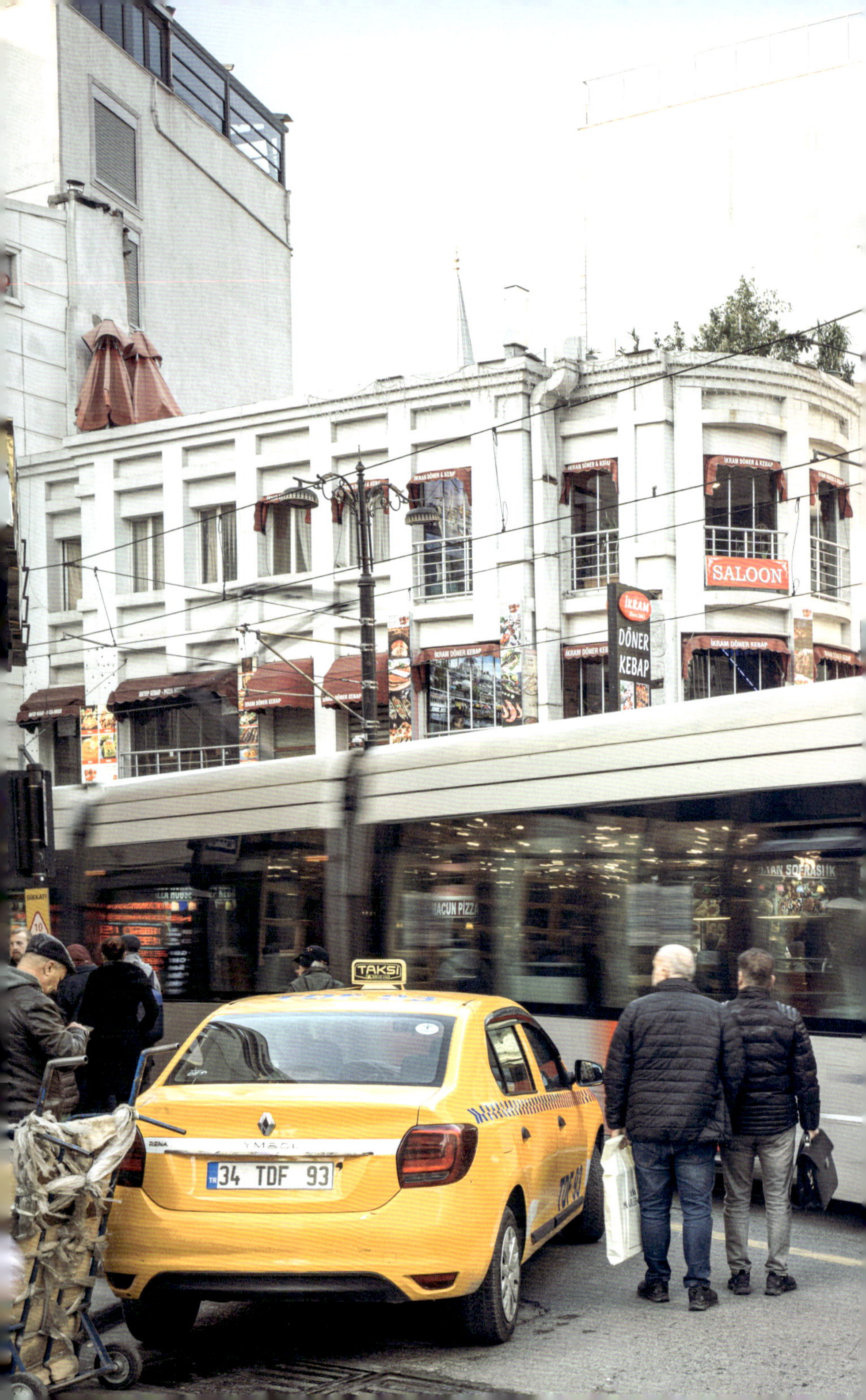
SALOON
İKRAM
DÖNER
KEBAP
TAKSİ
34 TDF 93

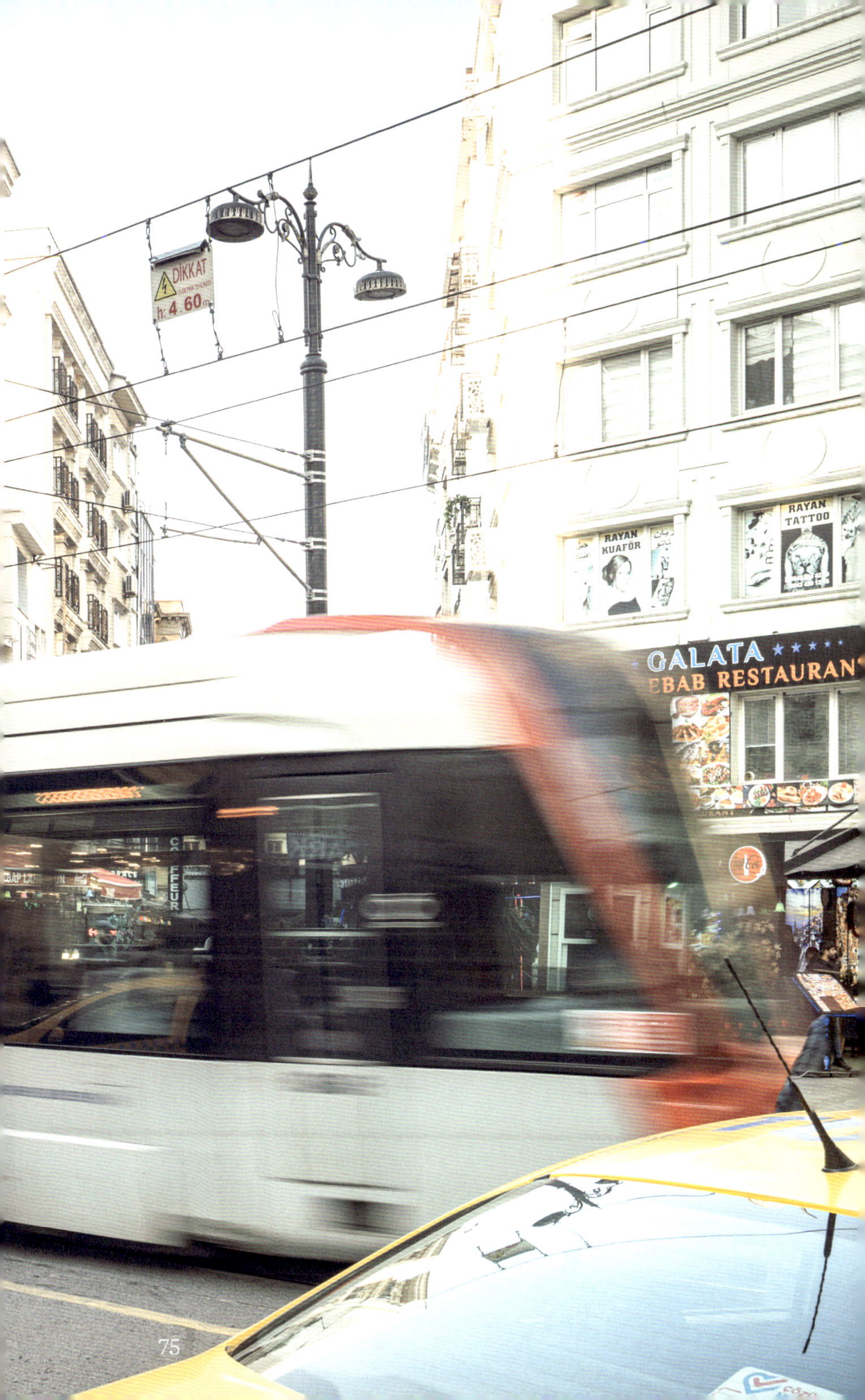
DİKKAT
h: 4.60m
RAYAN
KUAFÖR
RAYAN
TATTOO
GALATA
EBAB RESTAURAN

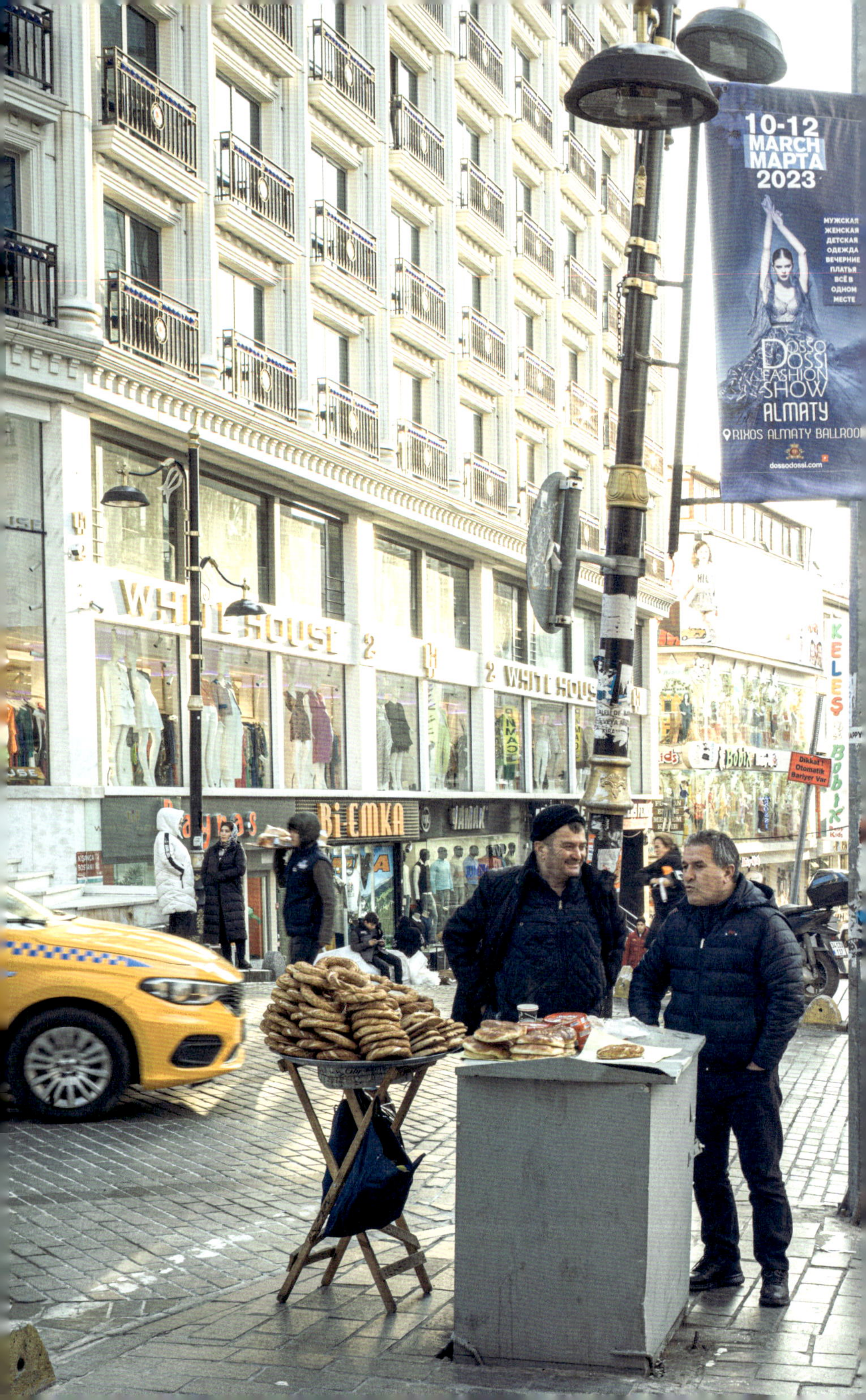
10-12
MARCH
МАРТА
2023
МУЖСКАЯ
ЖЕНСКАЯ
ДЕТСКАЯ
ОДЕЖДА
ВЕЧЕРНИЕ
ПЛАТЬЯ
ВСЁ В
ОДНОМ
МЕСТЕ
DOSSO
DOSSI
FASHION
SHOW
ALMATY
RIXOS ALMATY BALLROO
dossodossi.com
2 WHITE HOUS
Bi EMKA
Dikkat!
Otomatik
Bariyer Var
KELEŞ
Bobik

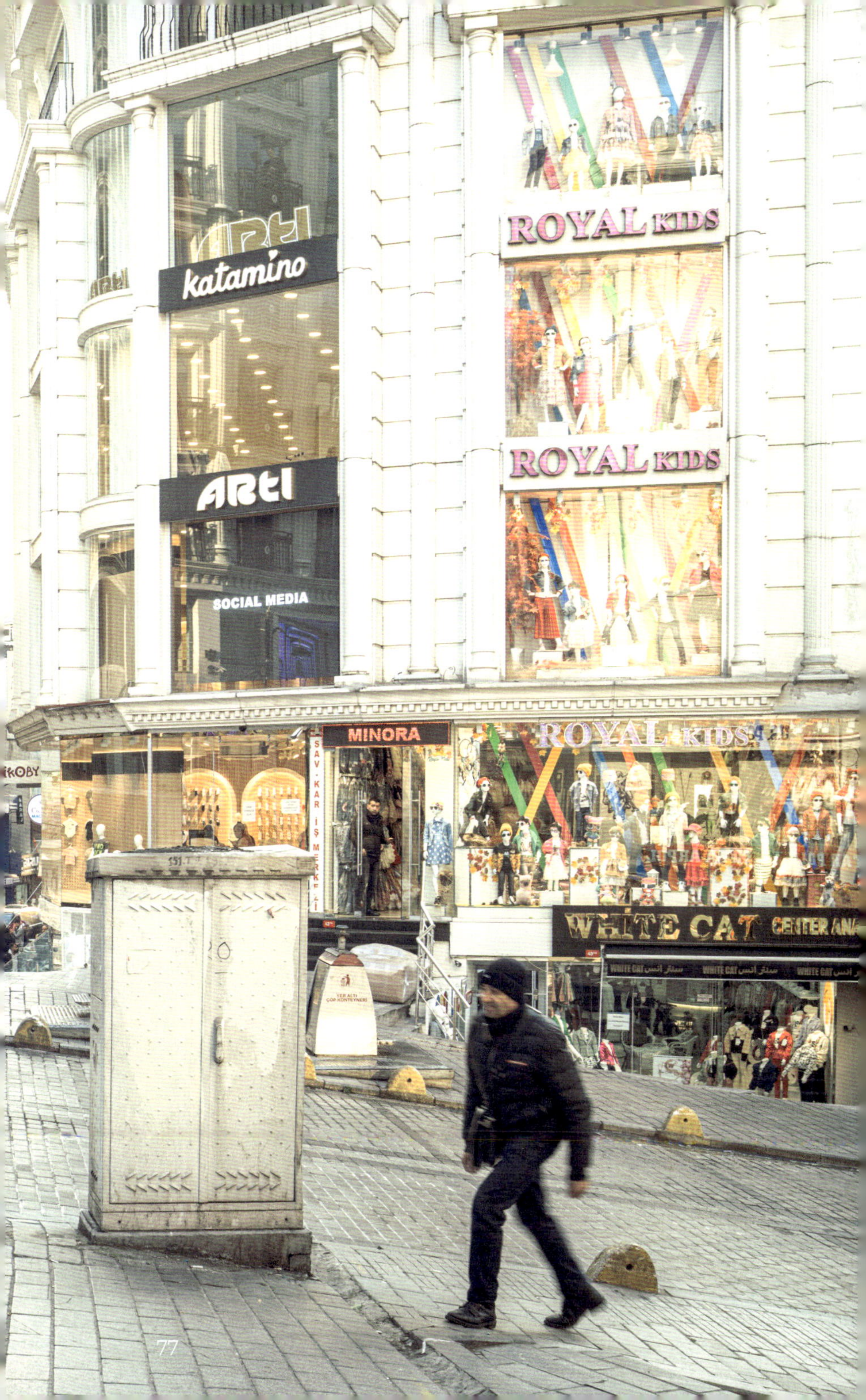
katamino
ARTI
SOCIAL MEDIA
ROYAL KIDS
ROYAL KIDS
MINORA
ROYAL KIDS
WHITE CAT
YER ALTI ÇÖP KONTEYNERİ

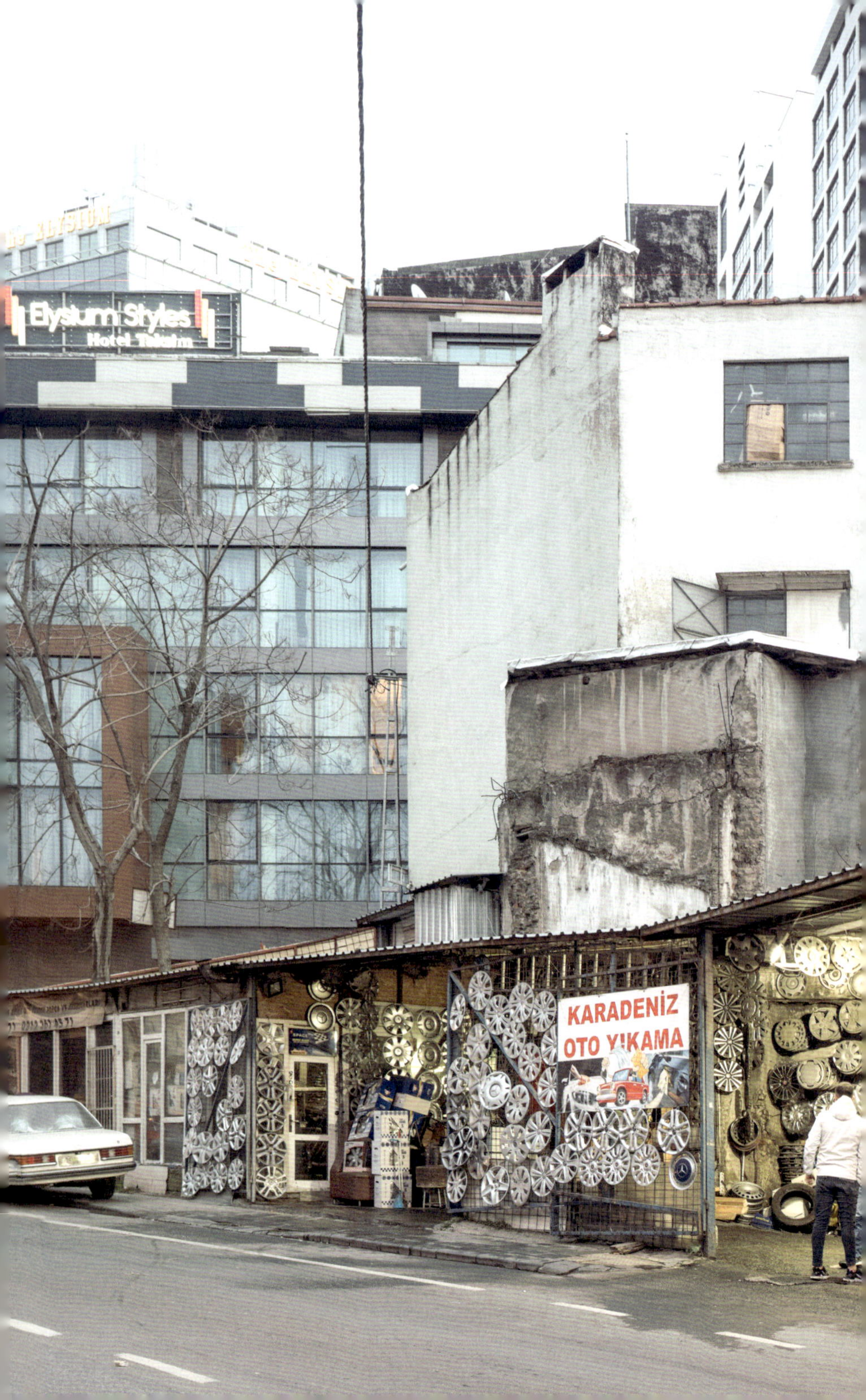
Elysium Styles
Hotel Taksim
KARADENIZ
OTO YIKAMA

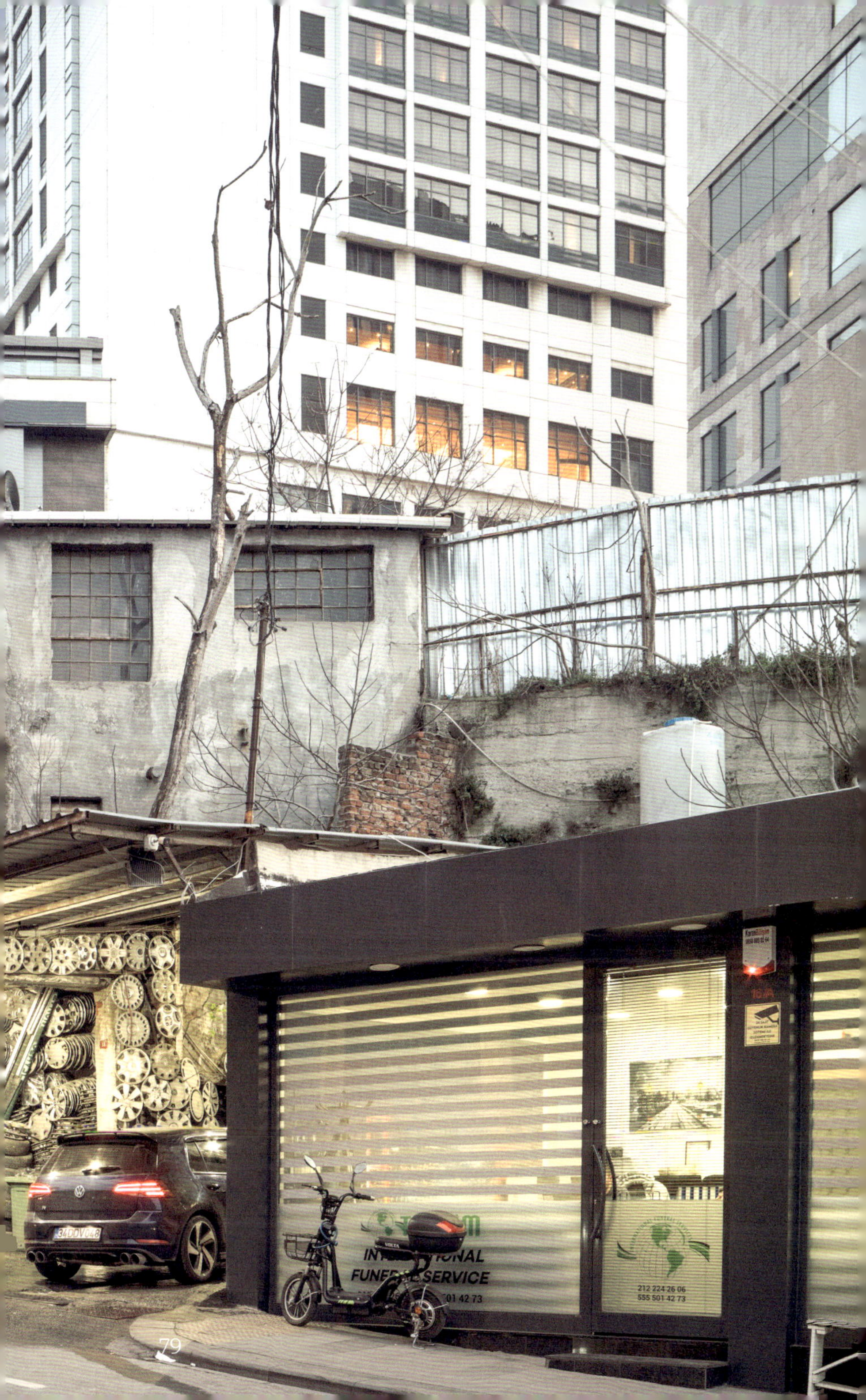
SERVICE
212 224 26 06
555 501 42 73

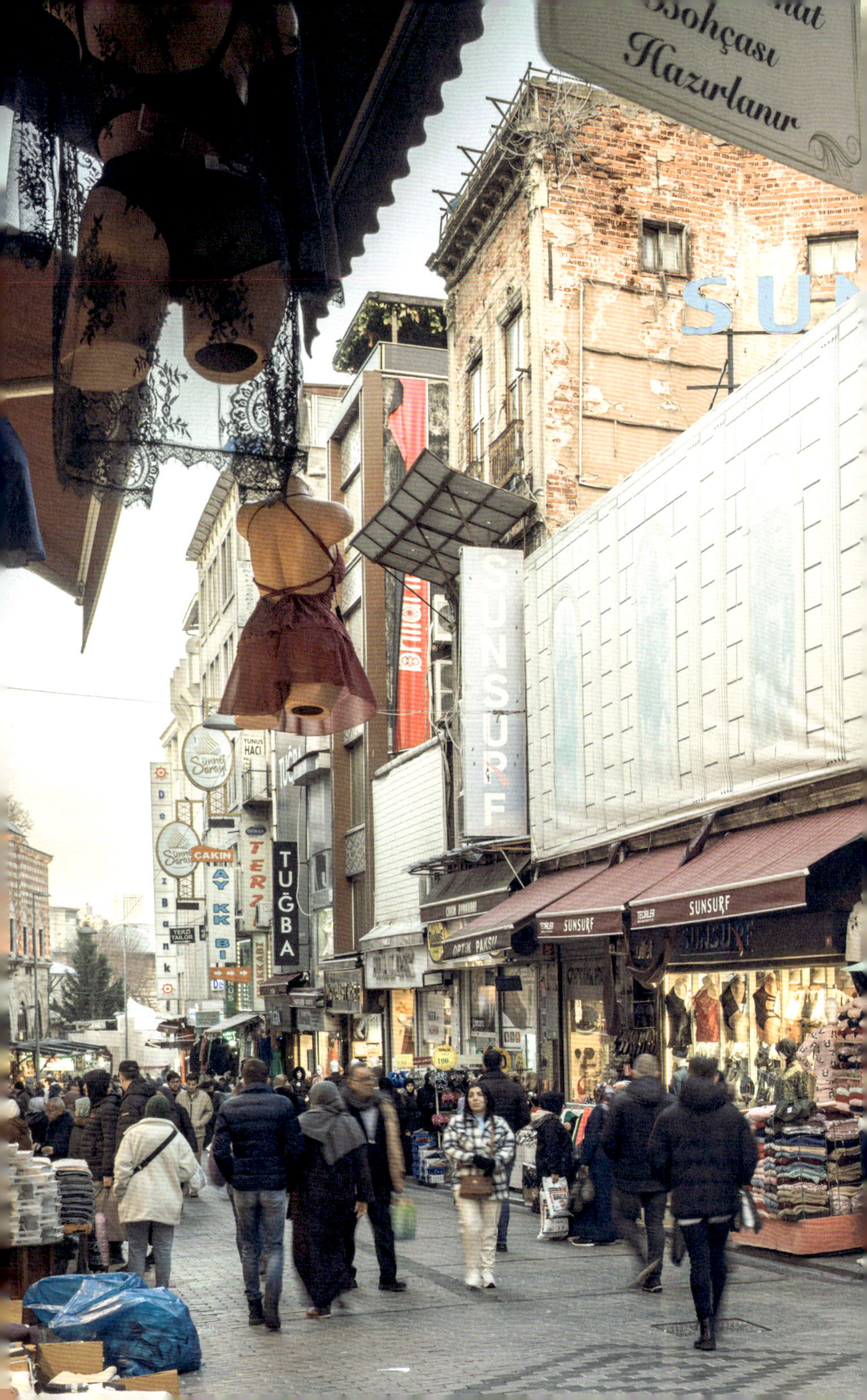

Hazırlanır
SUNSURF
SUNSURF
TUĞBA
OPTİK PAKSU
ÇAKIN
TUNUS HACI
TERZİ TAILOR

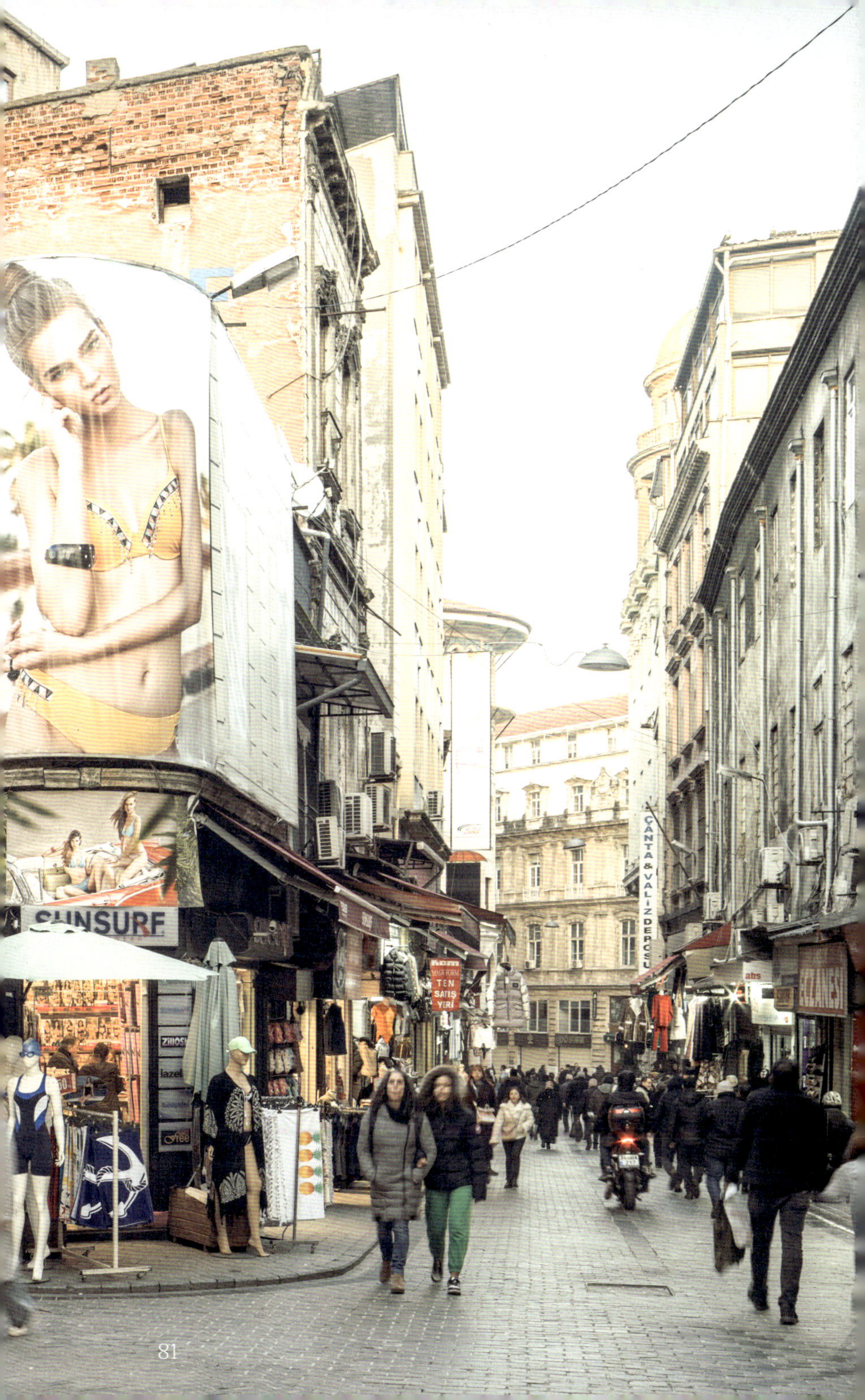
SUNSURF
ÇANTA & VALİZ DEPOSU
TEN SATIŞ YERİ

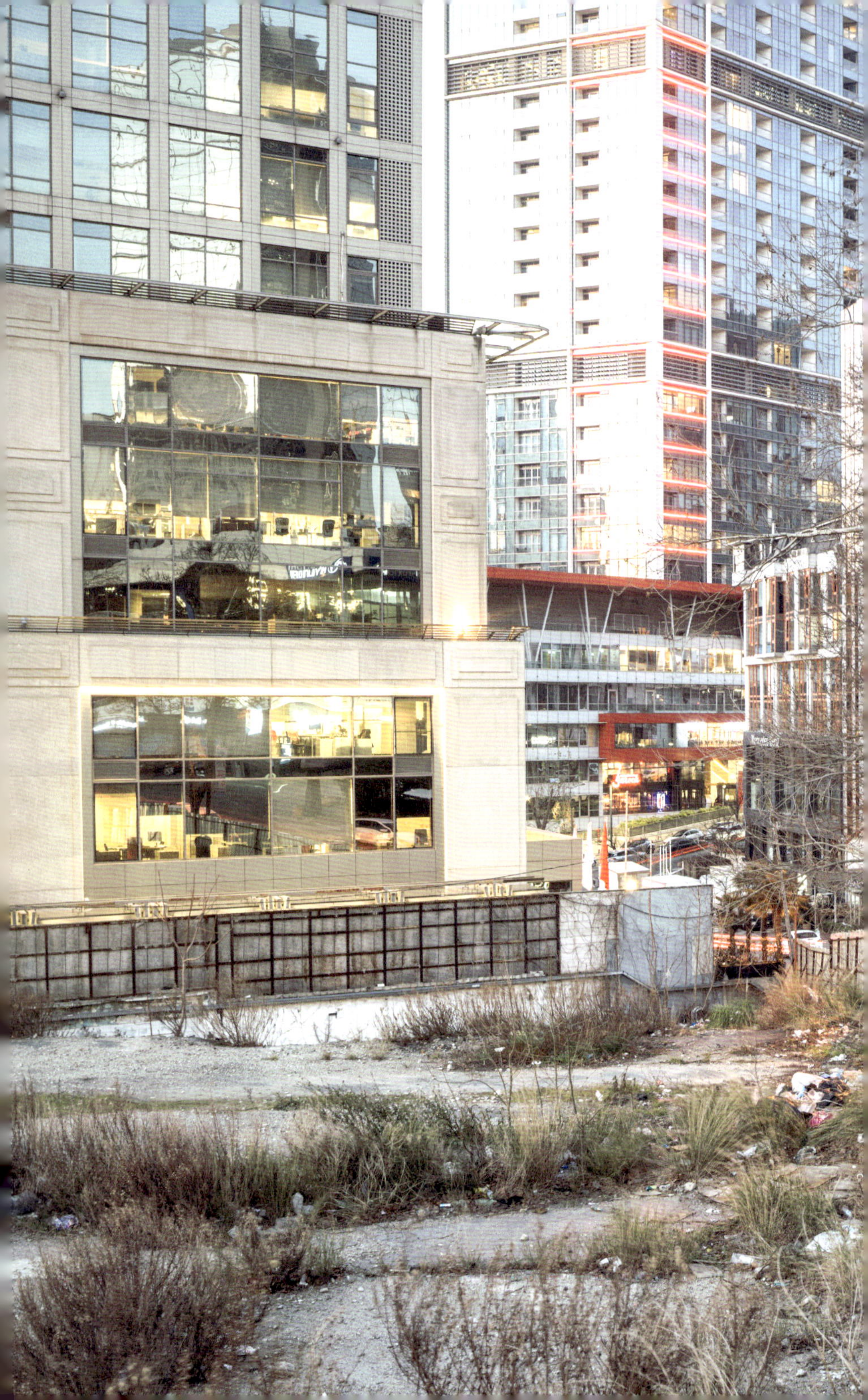

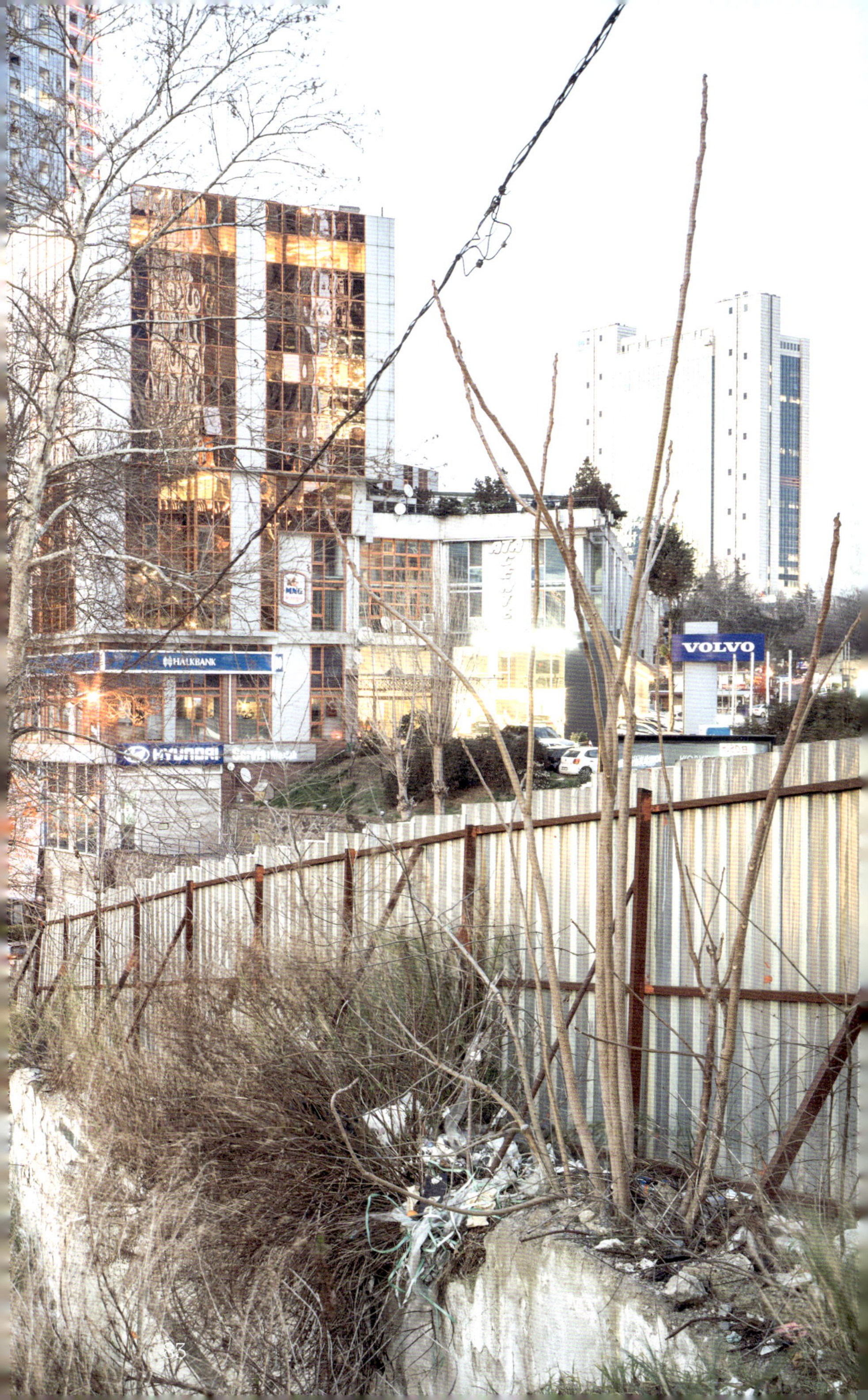
HALKBANK
HYUNDAI
VOLVO

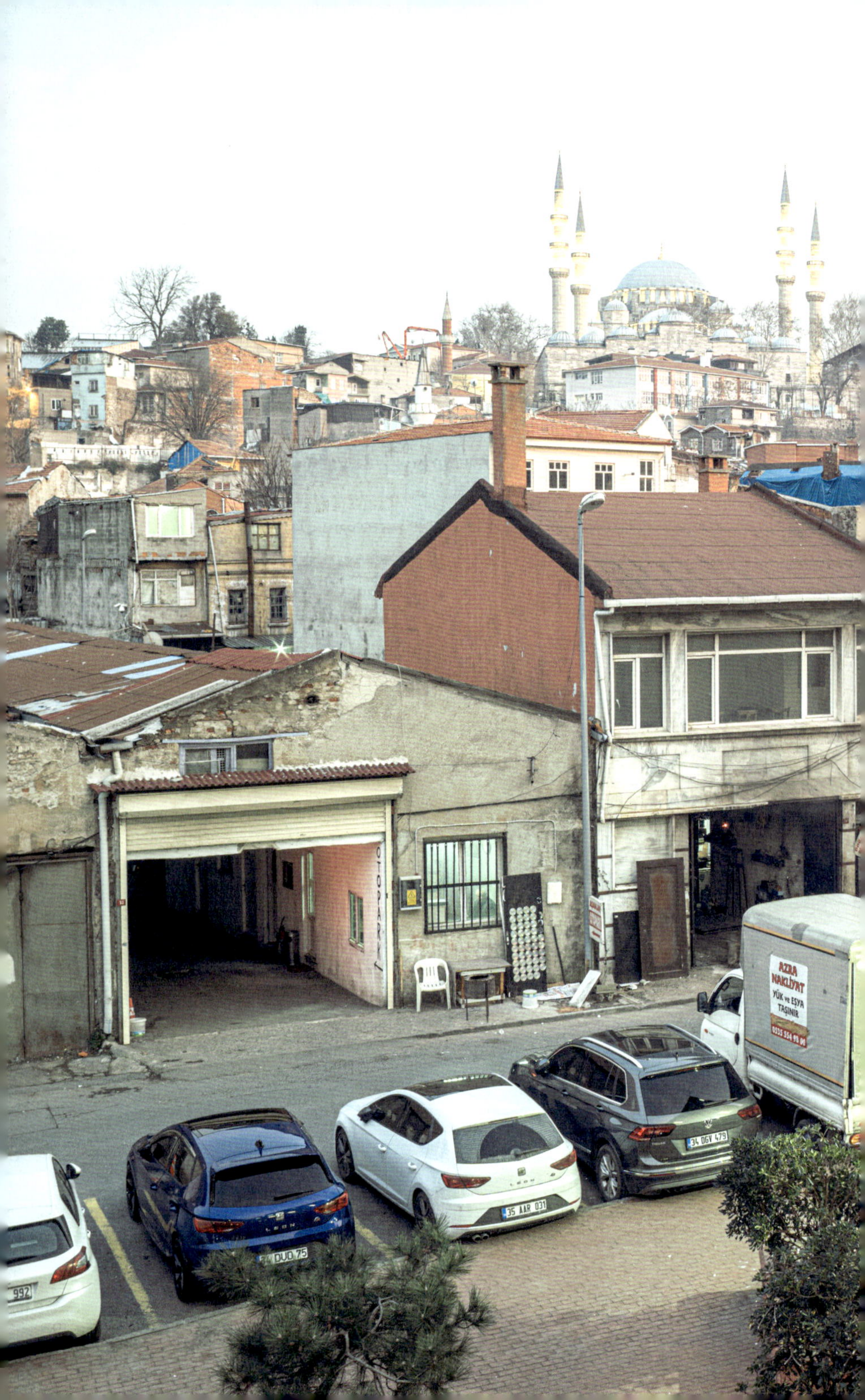
OTOPARK
AZRA NAKLİYAT
YÜK ve EŞYA TAŞINIR

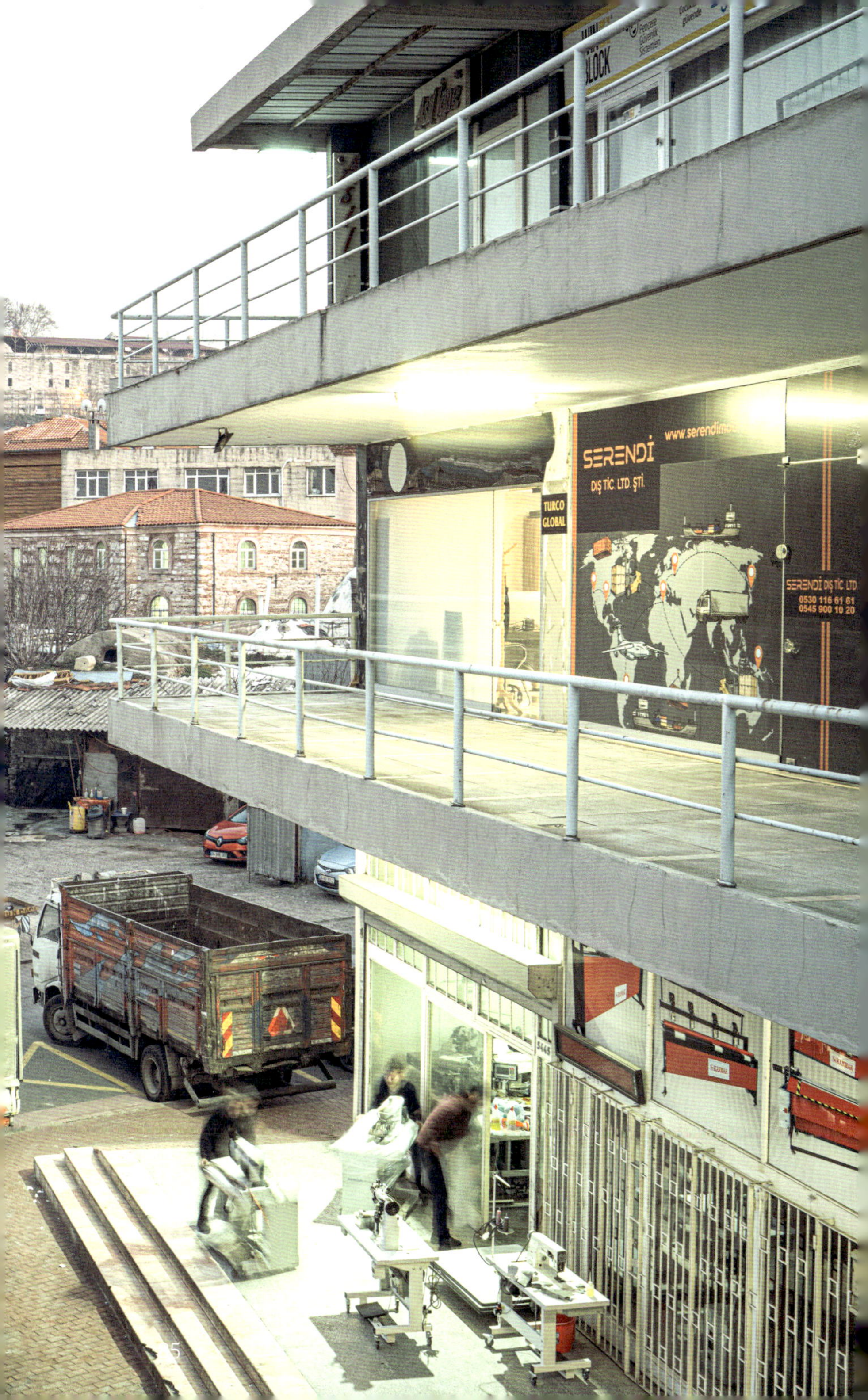
SERENDİ
DIŞ TİC. LTD. ŞTİ.
TURCO GLOBAL
SERENDİ DIŞ TİC. LTD
0530 116 61 61
0545 900 10 20

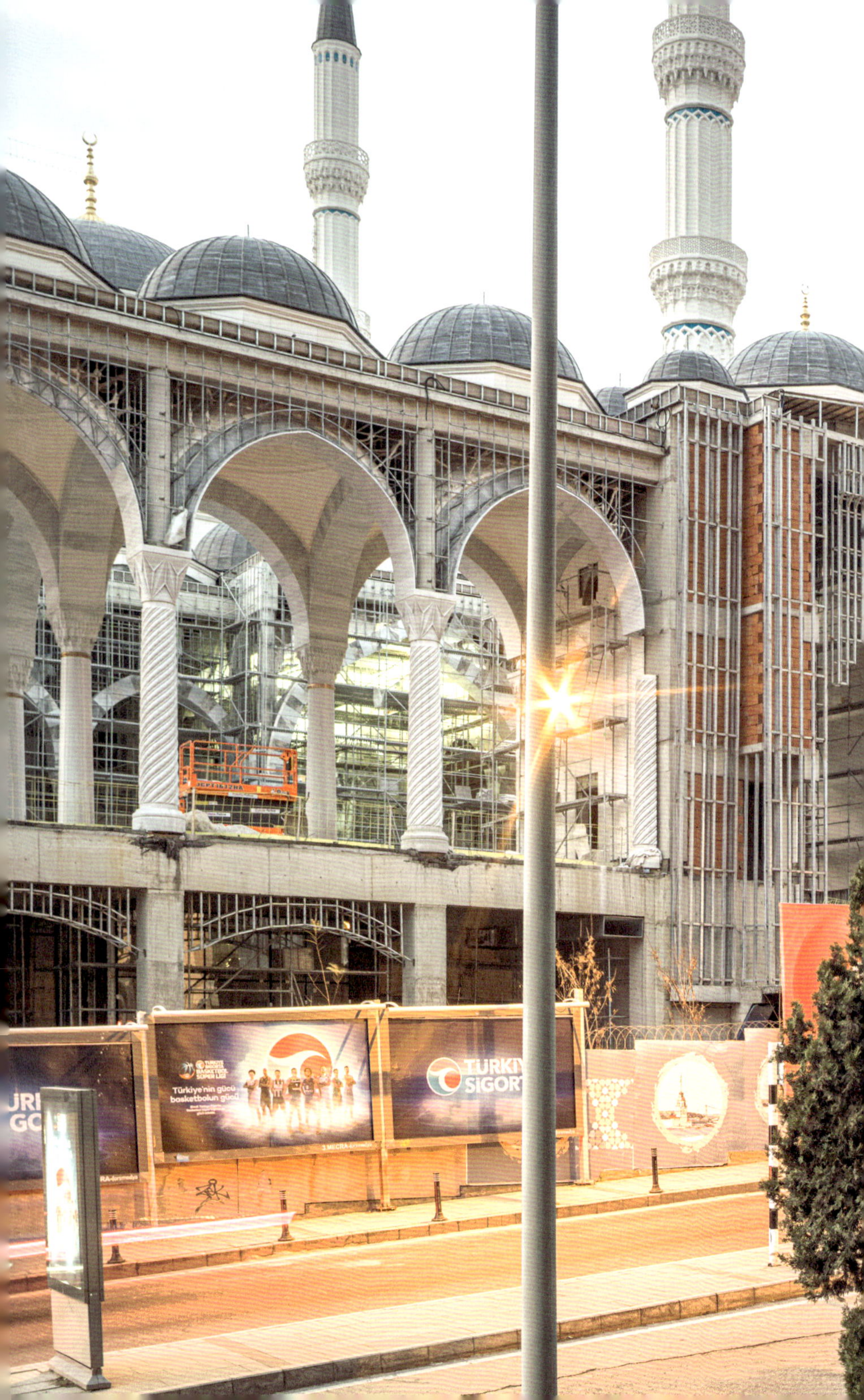
Türkiye'nin gücü
basketbolun gücü

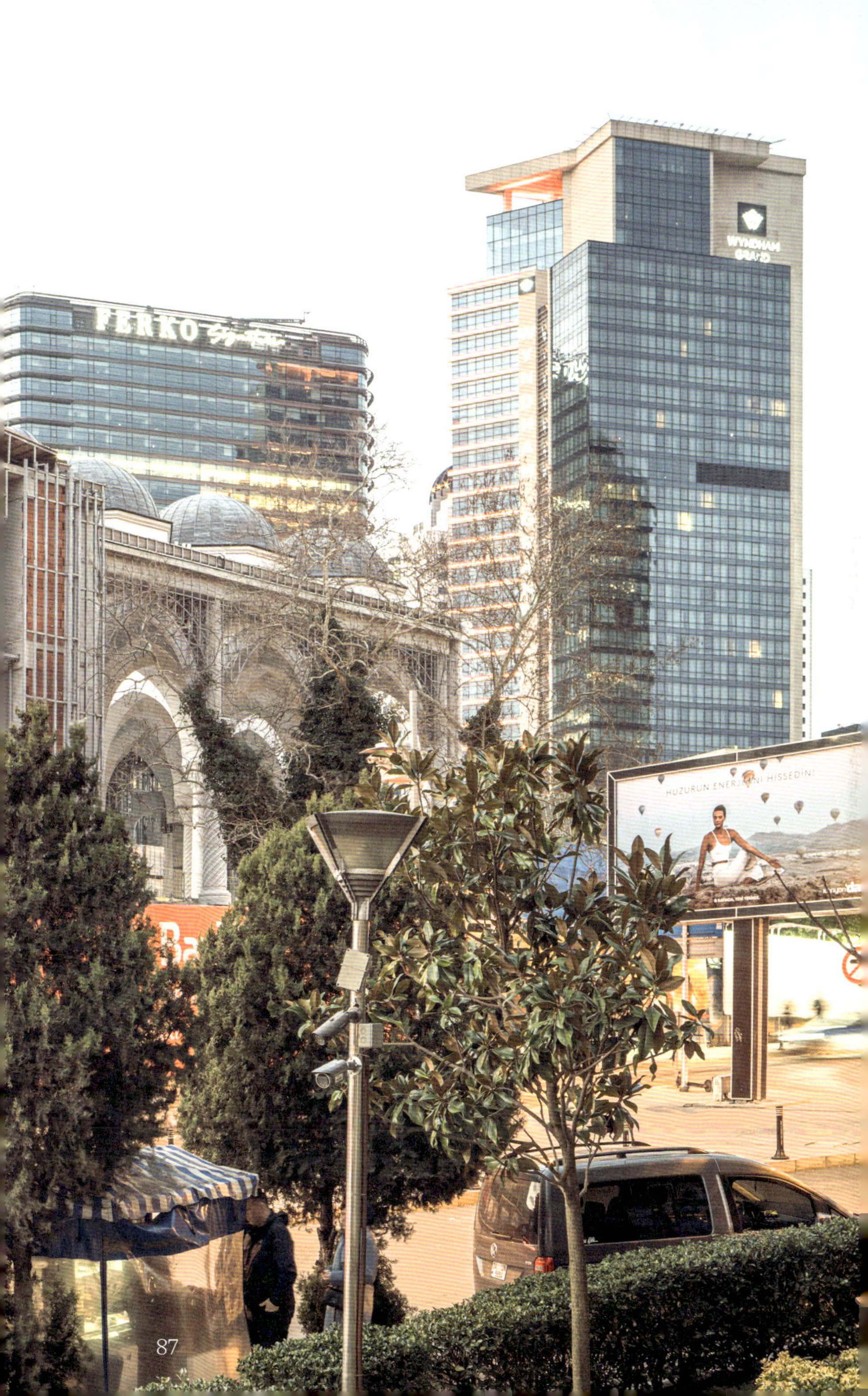
FERKO
WYNDHAM
GRAND

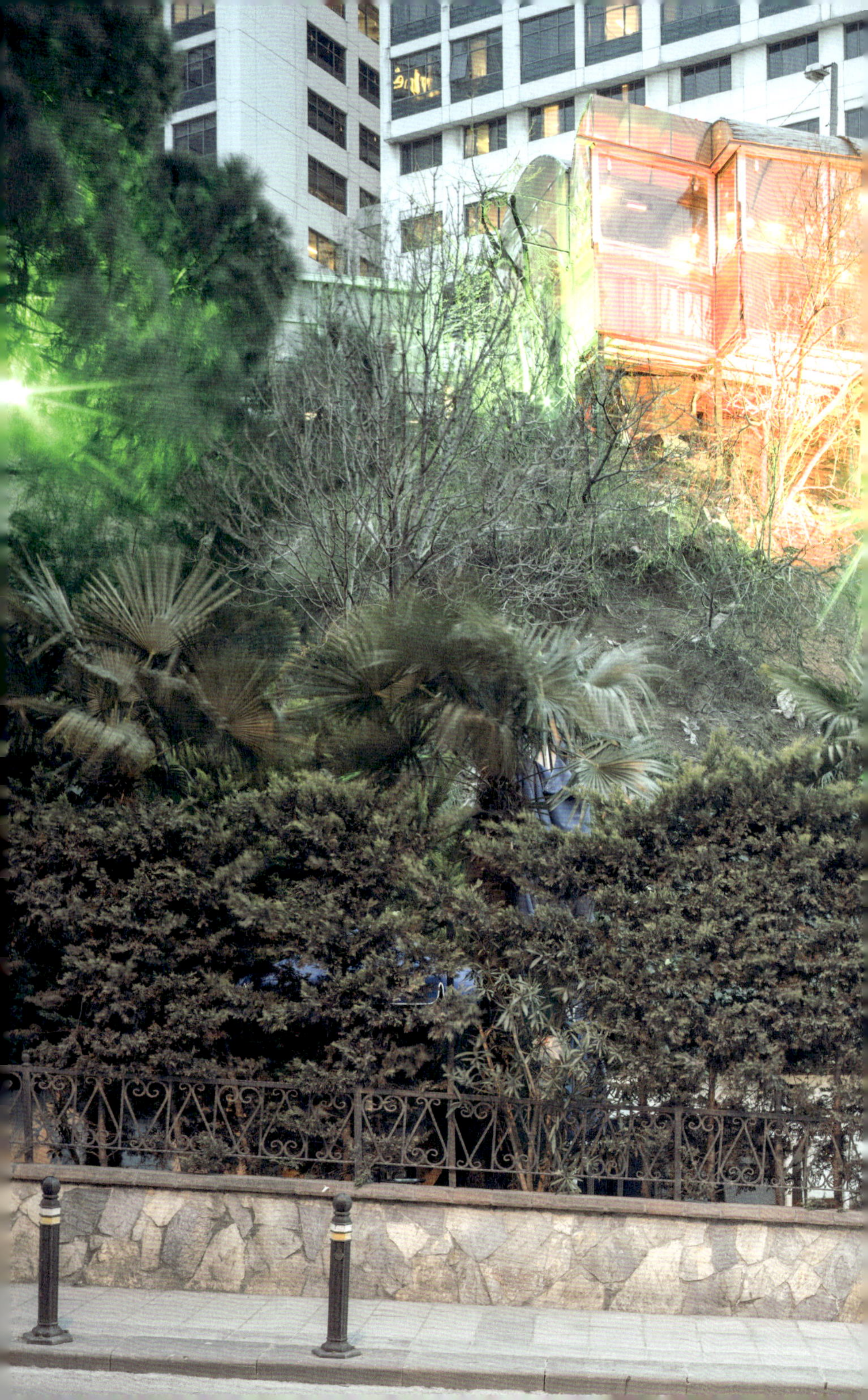

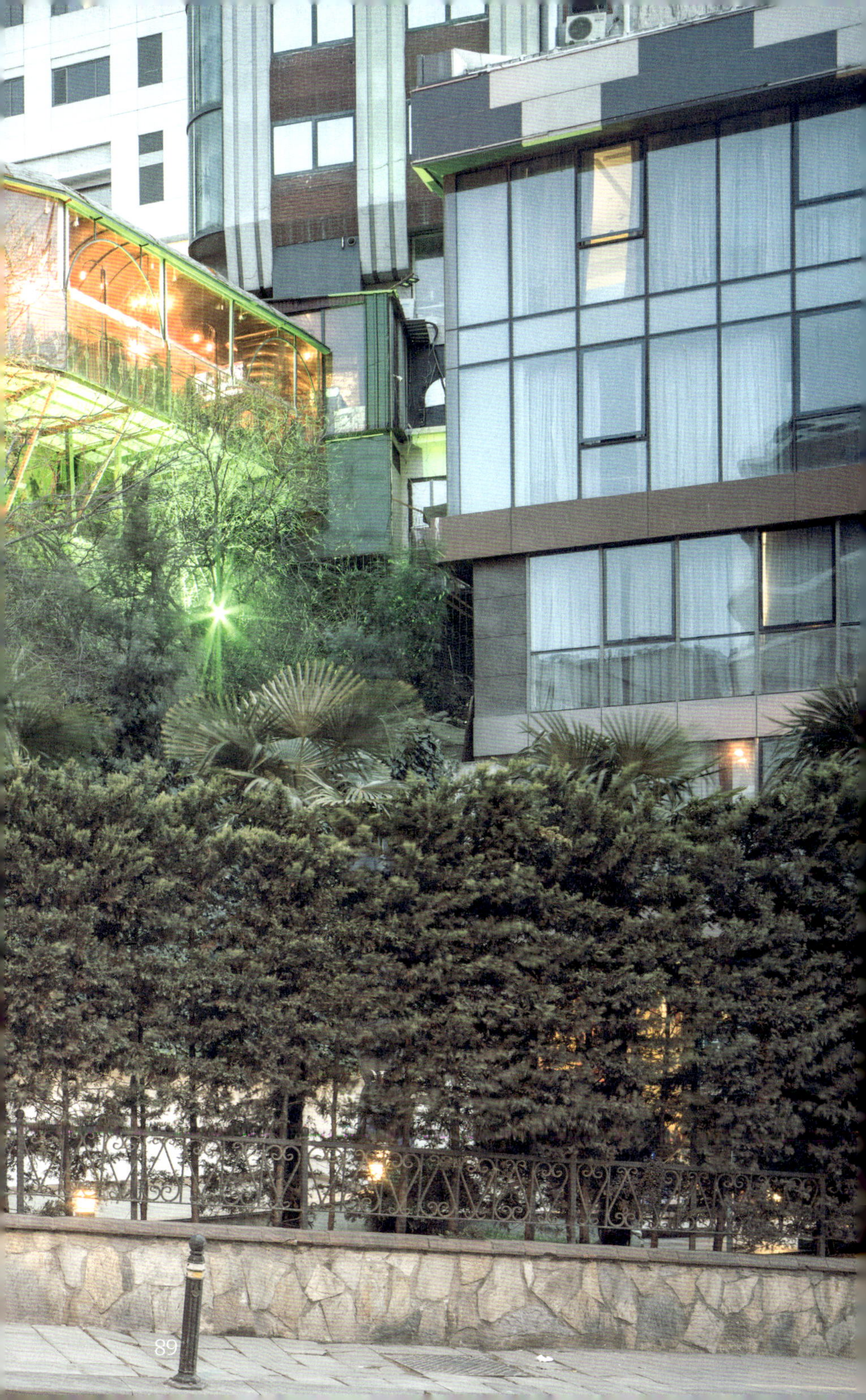

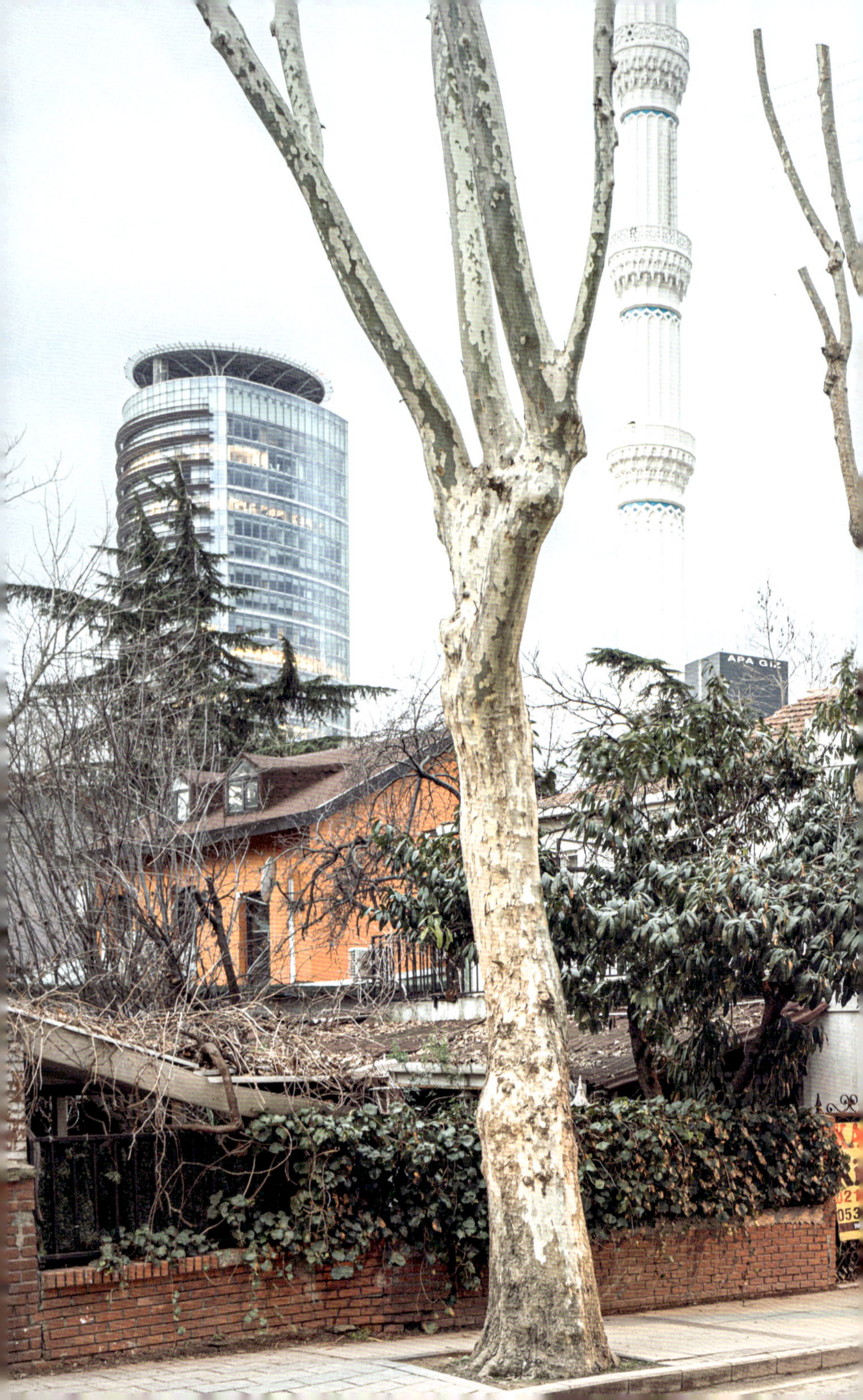
APA GIZ

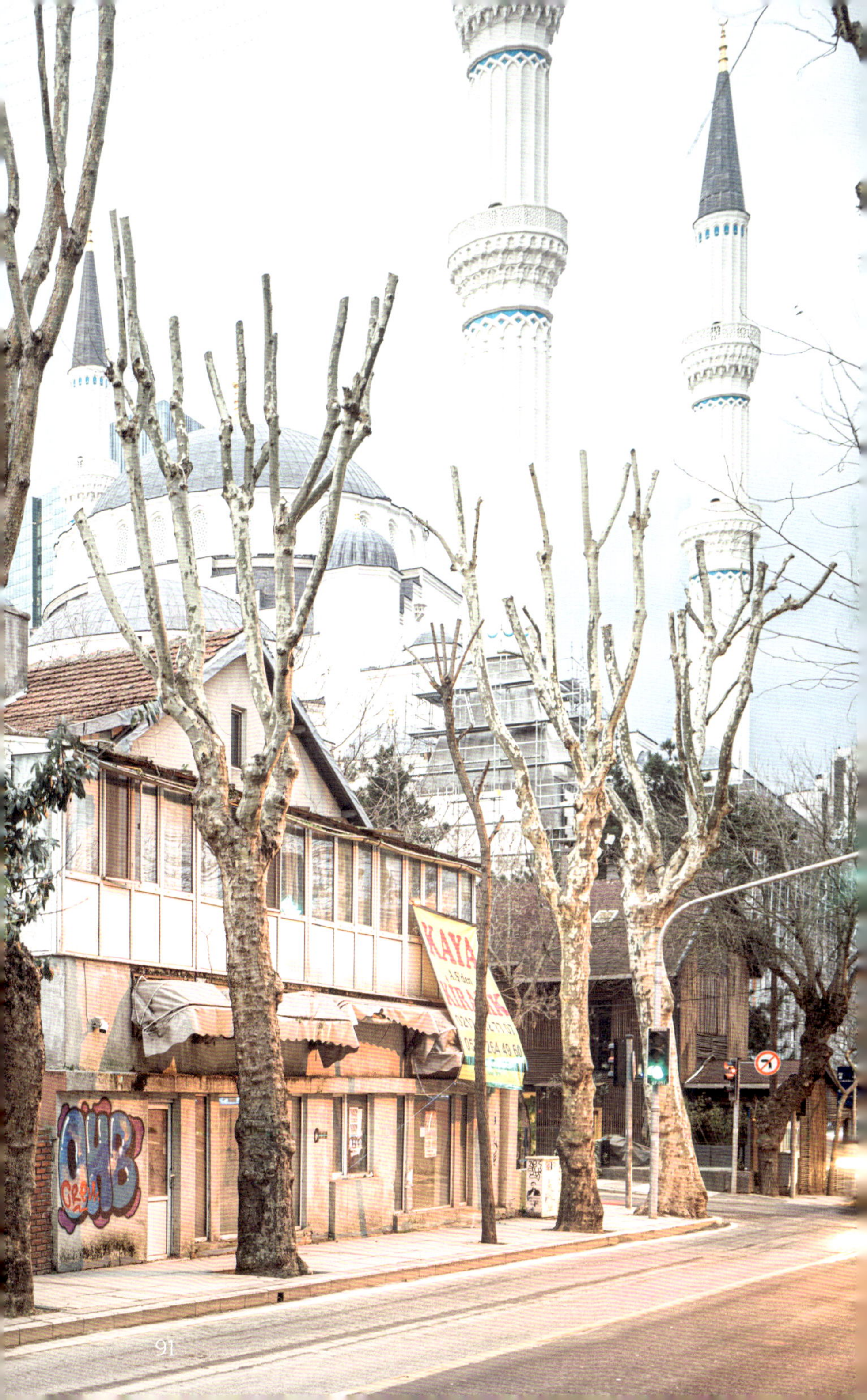
KAYA

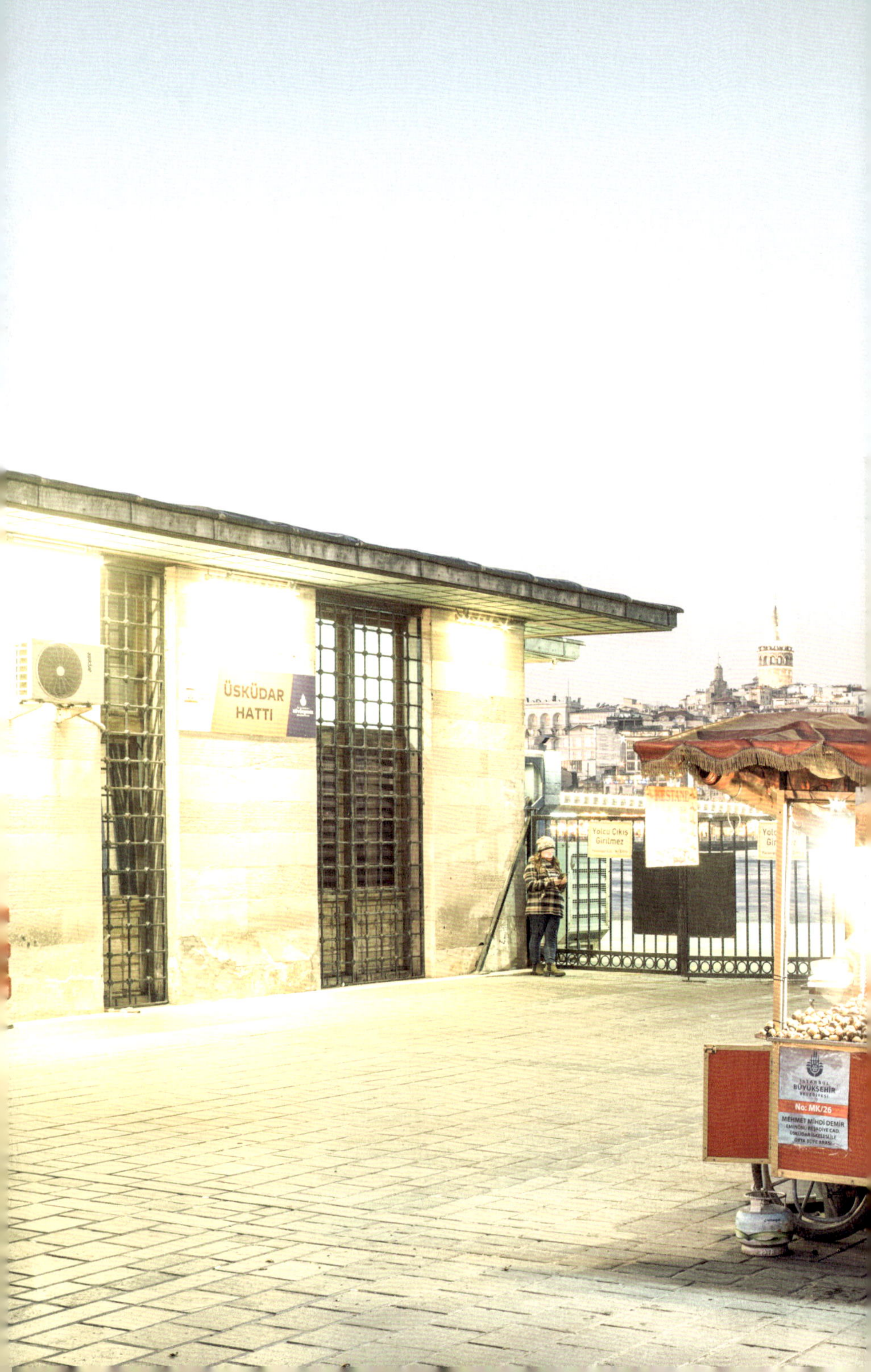
ÜSKÜDAR
HATTI
Yolcu Çıkış
Girilmez
İSTANBUL
BÜYÜKŞEHİR
BELEDİYESİ
No: MK/26
MEHMET MİHDİ DEMİR
EMİNÖNÜ REŞADİYE CAD.
ÜSKÜDAR İSKELESİ İLE
ORTA BÜFE ARASI

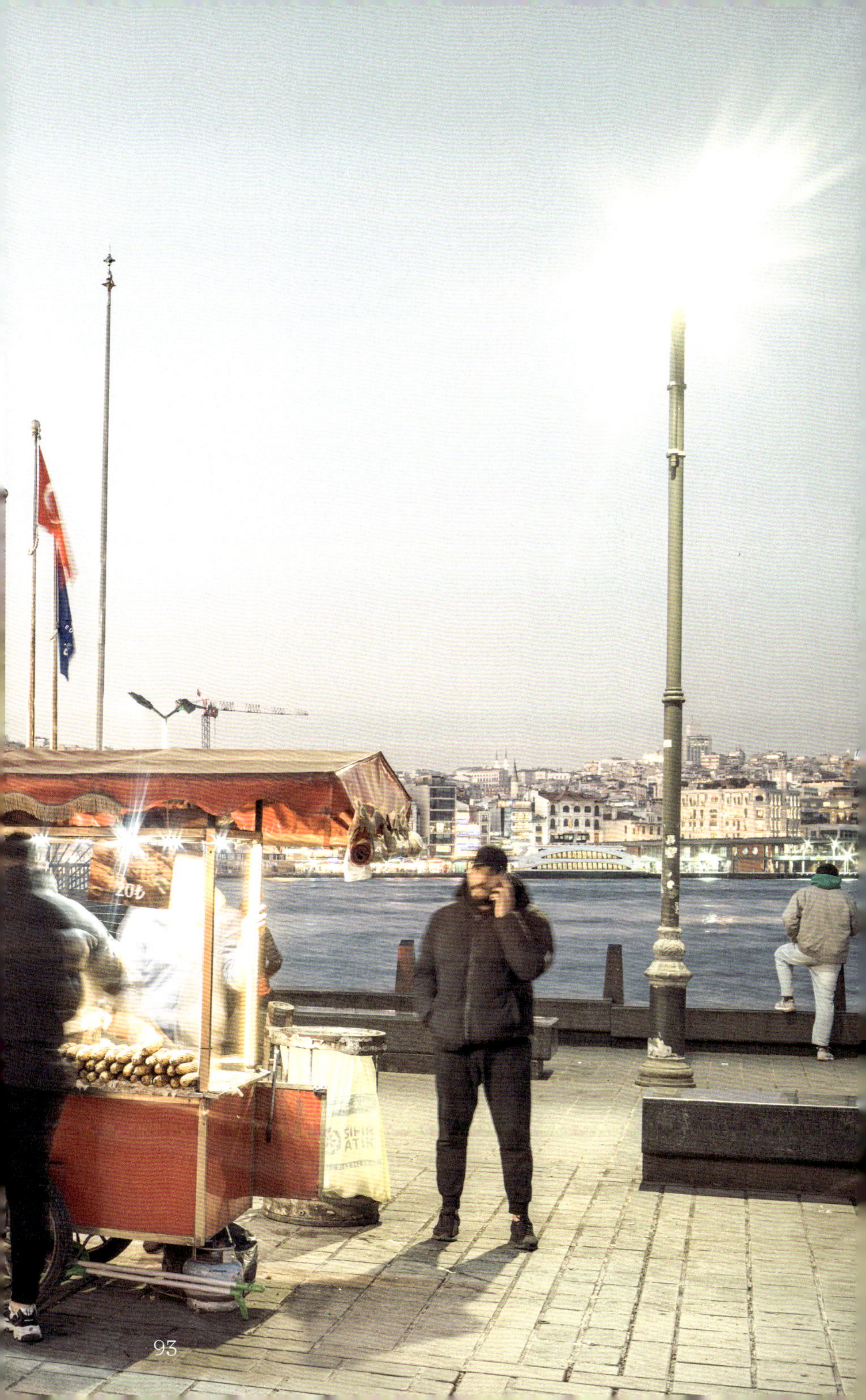
20₺

Previous Diaries

Cairo Diary #1
2014
ISBN 978-1-908889-20-1

Athens Diary #2
2015
ISBN 978-1-908889-29-4

Wolfsburg Diary #3
2016
ISBN 978-1-908889-34-8

Taipei Diary #4
2015
ISBN 978-1-908889-30-0

Kochi Diary #5
2018
ISBN 978-1-908889-44-7

Beirut Diary #6
2018
ISBN 978-1-908889-40-9

Wuhan Diary #7
2018
ISBN 978-1-908889-645

Zurich Diary #8
2019
ISBN 978-1-908889-65-2

Budapest Diary #9
2020
ISBN 978-1-908889-66-9

Osaka Diary #10
2020
ISBN 978-1-908889-56-0

Dhaka Diary #11
2021
ISBN 978-1-908889-86-7

Yangon Diary #12
2021
ISBN 978-1-908889-87-4

Minsk Diary #13
2021
ISBN 978-1-908889-88-1

Linz Diary #15
2021
ISBN 978-1-908889-90-4

The diaries listed above were published by *thevelvetcell.com* and are available on the website.

George Town Diary #16
2022
ISBN 978-3-96070-090-6

Unna Diary #17
2022
ISBN 978-3-96070-089-0

Sarajevo Diary #18
2022
ISBN 978-3-96070-088-3

Bangkok Diary #19
2022
ISBN 978-3-96070-087-6

Kuching Diary #20
2024
ISBN 978-3-96070-105-7

Turin Diary #21
2024
ISBN 978-3-96070-103-3

Wilson Diary #22
2024
ISBN 978-3-96070-106-4

London Diary #23
2024
ISBN 978-3-96070-104-0

New York Diary #24
2025
ISBN 978-3-96070-118-7

Vilnius Diary #25
2025
ISBN 978-3-96070-119-4

Istanbul Diary #26
2025
ISBN 978-3-96070-120-0

Norderney Diary #27
2025
ISBN 978-3-96070-121-7

The diaries listed above were published by *hartmann-books.com* and are available on the website.

Istanbul Diary
Peter Bialobrzeski

Published by
Hartmann Books
Liststraße 28/1
70180 Stuttgart
hartmann-books.com

Photographs
Peter Bialobrzeski
bialobrzeski.net

Graphic Design and Typesetting
Sarah Fricke, Distaff Studio

Copyediting
Tas Skorupa, New York

Printing and Binding
Gutenberg Beuys, Hannover

Paper
Magno Volume

Typefaces
ABC Diatype, GT Alpina

First Edition, 2025
500 copies

ISBN
978-3-96070-120-0

For Claudia